# GOOD GIRL

sound bites from an
intimate revolution

maureen fitzgerald

I share this story to exhale and shed light on the difficulties of life. I also share this to show we do not have to be shackled to our trauma.

There are magical possibilities that can emerge if we choose to really live.

Copyright © 2021 Maureen Fitzgerald Creations.
Copyright © 2021 Good Girl, sound bites from an intimate revolution.

All rights reserved. No part of this publication may be reproduced, distributed, or transmitted in any form or by any means, including photocopying, recording, or other electronic or mechanical methods, without the prior written permission of the publisher, except in the case of brief quotations embodied in critical reviews and certain other noncommercial uses permitted by copyright law. For permission requests, write to the publisher, addressed "Attention: Permissions Coordinator," at the address below.

ISBN: 978-1-387-84248-3 (Paperback)

Library of Congress Control Number: 2021924163

Front cover image by Maureen Fitzgerald.
Book design by Maureen Fitzgerald.
Chapter images by Maureen Fitzgerald.

Printed by, Lulu Press, Inc, in the United States of America.

First printing edition 2021.

Lulu Press, Inc.

www.momofitz.com

This story is a little different.

It's a collection of soundbites from my life:

poems, conversations, quotes, tabs, journal entries...

It is meant to be read from start to finish. Although, there are no rules, so feel free to jump around and sit with the ones that make you feel something.

There is a lot of white space. If you own a copy, please write, draw and scribble all over this. Interact and play with this if you so wish, or leave it blank, there is peace in simplicity.

This story could be potentially triggering for those with experiences with toxic relationships. Please be kind to yourself.

Thank you to the books, people, and places that have been a source of love when I didn't have it for myself.

To my friends and partner that waited patiently for me to realize my own worth.

To my family who showed up in ways I never expected.

To my therapist who was my lighthouse when I was completely, undeniably lost.

To my best friend, guardian angel, and copy editor, Carolynne.

Thank you to my editor, Joanne Sprott, you were so nice to me when I needed it.

To Linda Christensen and the Oregon Writing Project, without your mentorship I would have never believed I had anything to share.

Kelsey Hones, Tamika Abaka-Wood and my employer B+A, your support in documenting this story has been invaluable.

Robi Wood, my first reader and book sage.

To my sweet doggo, Migos who has been with me through it all, and for never letting me stay in bed too long.

And to the bad women who figured this out long before me.


Thank you.

## contents

a shattered illusion

personal delusions

spiritual transfusion

newfound effusions

human devolution

overwhelming confusion

reimagined conclusion

intimate revolution

**What is the difference between
a revolution and a rebellion?**

A revolution is a
rebellion you win.

For all the good girls.

# SHATTERED ILLUSION

## The Great + Powerful

I went to see the wizard

about filling my heart with love

He boomed through fire and smoke

grand gestures and warm vows

he held me close

and placed a yellow ring on my finger

and a ruby kiss on my lips

With the smile of a salesmen

he sold me a promise

that I would be loved

It was perfect.

Me, a young teacher,
spreading ideas of justice fueled by white privilege and guilt.

Latin America was a fascination.
I learned Spanish.
I indulged in the culture.
The rules felt different than those I grew up with.
There was life here.

Marrying a Mexican American
whose father walked across the border,
I awed at this American dream.

No one expected much of me.
I was a small kid.
I didn't win tackles or headers, nor score all the goals.
Somehow, quietly and then all at once I played for a crowd of 20,000.
A professional.
That one gorgeous summer, everyone knew my name.

He was a local prodigy,
the youngest person in his high school hall of fame.
Player of the year and a state champion.
A professional too.
In El Salvador, he almost died from malaria.
He almost died...
He came back from the dead
and devoted his life to serving children.

He was the trophy I would bring home to show my parents
what a good girl I was.

How deserving I was.

My life blinked from black and white to color when he said he loved me.

He told me I was different from everyone else:

I understood that life was about giving back to others.

He was persistent and all-encompassing.

He called me the love of his life, and then fiancée without even asking.

He introduced me to everyone that way after we ran away from the waves.

He kissed me as we overlooked the sprawling ocean.

Our future felt just as vast.

In a few weeks, I was hooked.

I told my diary that he was it.

A love bomb that felt like a fairytale.

We were to coach soccer and teach,

to brighten the lives of young people

the way we wished ours were.

We were married on a hot summer evening in the Oregon countryside.

The winery twinkled with tea lights and burgundy dahlias.

When I said my vows he kissed me before he was supposed to.

He yelled, "I do!" and the crowd delighted in his affection.

We were going to live happily ever after.

Oh what a high tower to fall from.

Diary entry

February 27, 2019

Month 7 of marriage

*Dear Universe,*

*I've asked for some pretty petty favors in the past, like a job or a place to live. This time I am asking for you to give him his life back. For him, ya know? He is nothing but a ghost right now and I know deep down the true him is begging and fighting to emerge. The addiction has this part of him suffocated. I hope and pray that you will use your forces to help him heal or at least allow him to heal himself. He deserves a beautiful life.*

*With love,*

*Maureen*

Who gets married
and smiles and laughs and says vows and parades around like they've won the fucking lottery knowing they have tricked a person into loving him, the facade of him, the bullshit of him?
Who gets married
and takes their wife's credit cards and charges hotels to disappear in and smoke meth and then tells her about it like a child who shat the bed? And when I tell him I'm concerned about finances he tells me, "That's such a white person thing to worry about."
Who gets married and disappears for days only to call in the middle of the night to come get him from his hell?
Who gets married and leaves their wife to move into their new home by herself, nowhere to be found? He was nowhere to be found. My dad asking, "Where's your husband?" And all I could do was shrug. I fucking shrugged it off, like he didn't abandon me.

# Addict

*noun.*

1. a person who is addicted to a particular substance, typically an illegal drug.

2. an enthusiastic devotee of a specified thing or activity.

3. my husband.

"Methamphetamine is a highly addictive street drug with a variety of forms and street names. The drug gives users a 'rush' that includes feelings of enhanced well-being, heightened libido, increased energy, and appetite suppression.

Psychological effects observed with methamphetamine use include euphoria, paranoia, agitation, mood disturbances, violent behavior, anxiety, depression, and psychosis. Cheaper than cocaine, its stimulant effects are also longer lasting. As the mood- and energy-enhancing effects of binging methamphetamine begin to wear off, users begin 'tweaking,' a term describing a dangerous combination of restless anxiety, irritability, fatigue, and dysphoria.

Further use of methamphetamine temporarily improves the symptoms and further reinforces the addiction. Eventually, after days of sleeplessness, users 'crash' into a nonrestful sleep."

- Mayo Clinic

February 27, 2019

Month 7 of marriage

*Face facts.*

*He has an addiction to meth.*

*I am choosing to be here.*

*I have unhappiness.*

*He has unhappiness.*

*The house is expensive.*

*I pay all the bills.*

**Friend**: Did you know he was using meth before the wedding?

**Me**: No, I just thought he had anxiety and depression like we all do.

"Authentic human interactions become impossible when you lose yourself in a role."

- Eckhart Tolle, *A New Earth*

## My roles

Wife—by law

Teacher—miserable

Friend—to whom?

Confidant—for an addict

Enabler—his crutch

Bank—hemorrhaging money

Punching Bag—I know it's not intentional…

November 16, 2018

Month 4 of marriage

*It just sort of feels like things are falling apart.*

Smoke + Mirrors

just another man behind the curtain

### The Master Plan

I will save him from his addiction.

I will bring back my husband.

If the girl is good enough, she will always save the broken boy.

> *- A Walk to Remember*
>
> *- Grease*
>
> *- Cruel Intentions*
>
> *- Twilight*
>
> *- 50 Shades of Grey*
>
> *- Crazy, Stupid Love*
>
> *- She's All That*
>
> *- Dirty Dancing*

Oh, that scene in *Dirty Dancing*, where Baby is in Johnny's cabin after her dad saves Penny from a botched abortion.

Johnny tells Baby that he is "nothing" and that he loves that she wants to make the world better. He tells her that she's brave for wanting to change the world.

Baby tells Johnny she is scared of losing him, and through her goodness, she saves him. Through her goodness, she finds love.

I have worshipped this scene since I was 15.

## Tab

Wedding ..................................................... $29,124

Car rides at 3 a.m. to pick him up .............. 12

House ....................................................... $319,000

Driving him to therapy............................... 4

Dog ............................................................ $500

Times I wanted to die ................................. 8

Hotel rooms for drugs................................ $4,879

Thank-you notes for the wedding gifts..... 128

**Dad**: From the outside it looks like a shit show.

**Me**: He has some mental health issues but he is going to in-person care next week so it will get better.

**Dad**: Okay to be clear, I don't give a fuck about him. I care about you.

When you let my dad walk me down the aisle and my mom cried, MY MOM CRIED, and I spent months getting ready, and all my friends were there, and my whole family who never comes to visit came, and you said you would love me,


YOU SAID YOU WOULD LOVE ME.

**Grey old lady at Al-Anon:**

His horns fit my holes.

I hate you in ways

that feel unmanageable


It comes out in fits of rage

in the morning—


screaming in my car

because there was nowhere else

for the anger to go, and

I couldn't show anyone that I didn't have it all together


sobbing into bed linens with

the lights off, and my phone off, wondering if pain is permanent


stormy voices

nightmares where I wake up sweating

drenched

like I have to shower immediately


And somehow I just want you to get better

## DJ Brain

Those ghostly scenes of laughter and

        exposed teeth are the broken record

                that repeats

                and repeats

                the sweetest part of the song

    those little tastes

           are enough to crave

       the bad parts too

"The pain body is an addiction to unhappiness.

Once unhappiness has taken you over, not only do you not want it to end, but you want to make others as miserable as you are in order to feed on their negative emotional reactions. "

- Eckhart Tolle, *A New Earth*

**Him:** I have trauma.

**Me inside:** SO DO I

AND I'M NOT AN EMOTIONAL TERRORIST.

His father was worthless. A smiling saint for the church, a do-goody community spectacle that tortures his family behind closed doors. The apple never even left the tree. What a horrible person. And he always said how he wasn't his father. He always said he wasn't him. He never wanted to be him.


His poor mother... Abused, imprisoned by that man's hands and words, and she still believes that God loves her. How? I would think God fucking hates me.


And I do.

Daddy Issues

I knew I had to leave him

when I looked at his mother

and grieved the life she never had

Remember when you told me my friends and family don't care about me?

Remember when you told me I was an alcoholic every chance you got because I got drunk once on my birthday.

Remember when you said that and you were getting high every week on meth and weed and drinking.

Remember when you told me I was wrong. All the time.

Remember when you told me it was my fault when male students hit on me.

Remember when you told me almost everything was my fault.

Remember when you told me to not come home.

Remember when you left when I finally did.

Remember when you tried to blow meth in my mouth.

Remember when you I covered for you coaching when you didn't show up.

Remember when you told me you didn't want my pussy and you definitely didn't want my ass.

Remember when you told me you got married because you knew I would leave if you didn't.

Remember when you told me you didn't want to get married in the first place.

Remember when you told me I was selfish.

Remember when you told me to move out. Then took it back, then told me again. Then told me that I was the only person you could confide in and I'd saved your life.

Remember when you told me that no one knows the real Maureen.

Remember when you made me believe I was unlovable.

February 5, 2019

Month 7 of marriage

*Love without joy can feel hollow.*

# Tab

| | |
|---|---:|
| Nightmares | 32 |
| Panic attacks | 2 |
| Minutes cried | 455 |
| Minutes explaining to people he is having some "health issues" | 324 |
| Games I coached for him and I had no idea where he was | 17 |
| Times he told me to move out | 3 |
| Times he didn't come home | 31 |
| Times he told me to not come home | 9 |
| Times he told other people I was the love of his life | 42 |
| Times he told me I forced this life on him | 29 |

"While those who live flat lives may avoid struggle, a well lived life involves throwing oneself into struggle, that large parts of the most worthy lives are spent upon the rack, testing moral courage and facing opposition and ridicule and that those who pursue struggle are happier than those who pursue pleasure."

-David Brooks, *The Road to Character*

**Me**: Well pain is the professor, ya know?

**Friend**: Ya but to a degree...

## Waiting for happily ever after

A high wake

of heavy waves

Me, the ragged rock

caught in a trying tide

Weathered and bruised,

I begged to be spit out

On the shore

I'll hopefully rest

and live for the day to see

Remember when you told me I had a sex problem.

Remember when you told your mom I had a sex problem.

Remember when you told me you were on Tinder just to talk with people.

Remember when you told me that my waist wasn't as skinny as your ex-girlfriend's.

Remember when you drove 100 miles per hour drunk at midnight and ran red lights and I begged you to stop.

Remember when you told me you were addicted to porn.

Remember when you told me you wanted to be a monk.

Remember when you told me that I didn't deserve to be greeted when I entered the room.

Remember when you told me you had a gun to your head in Mexico because the cartels thought you were your roommate... but it was you they were looking for wasn't it?

Remember when you neglected the dog and you dumped a can of corn into his bowl because you were high in the bedroom.

Remember when you left the dog in the car for hours because you were getting high with your friends.

Remember when you were supposed to take care of him and he got fleas and diarrhea.

Remember when you tried to take the dog and I told you no because I took care of him and paid for him and his food and the vet and I'll call the cops if you take him and you told me that was SO white to call the cops.

**My Ego:**

You got skinny and

new clothes and

your hair done and

you're still not enough.

Here you are with your house,

the thing that you thought

would help him, and

you're still alone....

**Me:**

I just want the pain to stop.

## Cravings

Nothing

satisfies better

than the approval

of your oppressor

Remember when I told you that you were being mean and you told me you wouldn't have to be that way if I was just "better."

**Me:** I just know he's in so much pain. He has a lot of trauma.

**Therapist**: He is willing to risk his life for meth just like you are willing to risk your life for codependency. Codependency is your addiction.

August 21, 2019

Month 13 of marriage

*He came home and was all upset because Scout and Jose said, "How the fuck did you get so lucky to be with Mo?" and he said he had to "bite his tongue to not talk shit about me." Then proceeded to tell me I'm not real with my friends. I said I had a very honest conversation with Scout yesterday about my stuff and he was like, "When did I say Scout? Now you're just making stuff up".... He kept coming back to how I'm not honest and I said, "Oh, cuz you hate me." And he said, "No, I intensely dislike you." So I asked him what he hoped to achieve from this conversation. Then he just stopped.*

*I almost said, "Well lucky for you cuz I'm moving out in two days." I just have to make it two more days....*

December 30, 2018

Month 5 of marriage

*IDK why I am so messed up. Nothing of significance really happened unless I am suppressing it. I think I just have the right combo of mental issues. I really need to go back to therapy. I am eager to get to the bottom and root of my problems, my lack of confidence and feeling unlovable and alone. I thought I was doing way better too. I also am just generally afraid.*

## Please

Don't ask me why I didn't leave sooner

I believed in his goodness

I'm just trying not to hate myself for it

**Friend**: If there was one moment that sort of defined the relationship, what would it be?

**Me**:


**Me**: That's the worst part about it. There was no sweeping moment where I knew I had to leave. It was death by a thousand cuts.

I used to think the most powerful force in the universe was love.

Now I know that's wrong.

It's meth.

Friend:

If you

are climbing

a ladder

and you

offer your

hand to

the other

person

and they

don't take it

keep going

## Tab

Movers ...................................... $325

Deposit for new apartment ............ $400

New bed ................................... $440

Table and chairs .......................... $100

Rent..........................................$1650

## Ditched work to cry on their couch

It wasn't telling my parents that my marriage was ending that broke my heart.

It was telling my parents I couldn't hold it together anymore.

(An unsent letter)

Dear      ,

I've been thinking about us. Us the couple and us the individuals. We've been pretty sick huh? And at least speaking for myself our marriage seemed to exacerbate my feelings of inadequacy and unlovability. Notice I said, our marriage. The last thing I wanted from all this was for us to become more miserable than we were by ourselves. I have begun to heal and it is clear that marriage is the last thing either of us should be worrying about. My priority now is to heal and love myself as should yours. I said in my vows that I would vow to be my brightest self that you could be your best in return. Truthfully, I can't shine bright when I feel like I have to take care of you and prop you up and take on the brunt of your pain. I've been trying to control you and my own life instead of just listening.

I need to heal.


With love,

Maureen

Acceptance

that someone is lost in addiction

is acceptance of their death.

That person no longer exists.

They are never coming back.

August 24, 2019

Month 13 of marriage

*How ironic that this is the last page of my journal and the first night in my apartment away from him. All I can think of is "I open at the close." I have a lot of different thoughts and feelings. I'm sad, scared, hopeful. Sad that we had to separate. Scared to be back in Portland with just myself. I haven't allowed myself to really trust myself.*

*I got a text from my dad saying he was really proud of me and that he's always admired me. I don't know how to fully accept that. Probably because he never actually seems satisfied. But I inherited that mindset too—don't trust anyone, be humble to the point of paralysis. What would my dad be proud of? What can I be proud of?*

*I guess I am proud of myself for the strength I have demonstrated and the grace to see past this man's behavior and understand that he has a disease.*

*Email sent to him.*

Dear    ,

It is difficult to deliver this news as this is the last thing I ever wanted to happen to us. I have filed for divorce in order to continue my healing journey. You should be receiving a letter in the mail at your apartment.

It is important to me that you know that I love you deeply and want nothing but for you to be healthy and thriving with self-love.

It is also important to me that you know that this decision was not made lightly as this was not the life, and I can only assume for you as well, had envisioned for us.

I am retaining hope for our future as individuals in our respective healing. As best as I can I will always choose to love and see you through my heart.

With love,

Maureen

*Email back from him.*

FYI I do not receive mail at this address. Please send it to my parents.

Sent from my iPhone

Remember when you told me you were confused when I asked for a divorce.

## Selective Memory

Forgive me

for forgetting

there was a we,

like I forgave you

when you forgot to love me


Forgive me

for never forgetting

a deep cry of regret

when I think about

drowning

in the ruthless tide of you

# Shrapnel

What now?

# PERSONAL DELUSIONS

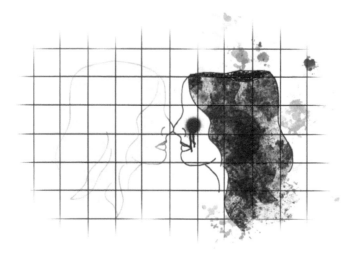

"Suffering has a noble purpose: the evolution of consciousness and the burning of ego... the light of suffering becomes the light of consciousness."

- Eckhart Tolle, *A New Earth*

## Simple requests

Find my own sense of belonging + security in the world

Work in a way that is meaningful to me and others

Have intimate, honest relationships with my friends and family

Be in a supportive, loving, honest, respectful romantic relationship

Strengthen my relationship with God

Travel + get to know the world better

Love myself unconditionally

Meditate more

Be less anxious in social settings

Exercise daily

Appreciate all I have, gifts, internal + external

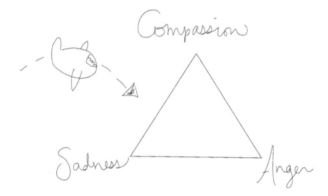

Bermuda Triangle of Grief

*December 31, 2018*

*Month 6 of marriage*

*I have a great life. I don't understand why my mind manipulates me into everything that is wrong all the time. "Which goggles did you put on today?" is what I should really ask myself. Look at my life:*

*Loving husband*

*Great friends*

*Beautiful house*

*Solid job*

*Supportive family*

*Why shouldn't I be thankful for all those things?*

# Conformity

perfectionism is

having your life so

orderly

and desirable

by the

market's standards

no one will notice

you're unworthy

Spiral text (reading from outside inward):

Deep down do I believe I deserve this? Was this God's plan to enlighten me? Does God hate me? Did I deserve this? Did my brokenness attract a broken person? Did I choose these toxic relationships? Did I hate myself?

Wheel of Torture

**Dad:** You can't keep blaming yourself...

He didn't just have you fooled, he had himself fooled.

# Tab

Nightmares.................................................................................... 43

Panic attacks ................................................................................ 13

Minutes cried ........................................................................... 1516

Minutes explaining to people the relationship was toxic ................ 980

Times I moved homes in a year ......................................................... 5

Times I said no to anything social ................................................... 364

Number of people telling me they thought there were red flags and didn't say anything because it "wasn't their place".................................... Everyone.


Because secretly, we all believe that this is what women deserve.

In Greek mythology, there is a story of a man named Icarus. His father was a master craftsman who gave him wings made of wax and feathers to escape Crete.

He was instructed not to fly too close to the sun.

Icarus ignored this wise advice, likely because he was arrogant and brash.

As he flew closer and closer to the sun, his wax wings melted and he fell out of the sky and drowned in the sea.

Look out for those wax wings.

Remember when I told you to never contact me again and you did it anyway.

Remember when you called me and told me there was Covid in the flu shots.

Remember when I had to block your number and you got a new number and texted me and I blocked you again.

Remember on what would have been our anniversary, our wedding song was playing outside the windows of my apartment complex.

Remember when you told me I was missed and if I wanted to talk to let you know.

Remember when I never let you know.

Remember when you were too busy to sign the divorce papers.

Remember when you called me and told me you were going to kill yourself because of what I was doing.

Remember when I had to plea for a decision from the judge to call it.

sometimes I wonder if my whole life was always going to blow up

if I was just chasing the dream of what I thought it meant to a good woman

a palatable woman

a deserving woman

it's like this shining stagnant target we all move towards

I don't know. The divorce club is pretty small at 28

it's not that I'm damaged goods

I'm just                                      different now

less shackled by rules


but more governed by bitterness

## Manufactured Housing

What about the things

we choose

to worship

and the systems

we

choose

to trust

like a North Star

that couldn't be further

from guiding us home?

**There are no rules +
the points don't matter**

I thought if I smiled and was kind,   I thought if I was never angry or mean
and was decently fit   and wasn't too fat
and reasonably clever   and was unremarkable
and well liked   and never pissed anyone off
then life would be easy.   then life would be fair.

**Me**: ya we're separating, he just had a lot of mental health issues he needed to address

**Friend**: omg, I'm so sorry this is happening

**Me**: ya well, I was broken too

**Friend**: what do you mean?

**Me**: well you don't marry a drug addict unless you're really sick too

Pain bells—

they keep ringing

like the carnival game

life and her hammer

are pulling an all-nighter


"Shhhhh be quiet"

I say.

Pop another prozac.

Take another shot.

Buy another dress.

Bring home a golden boy.

No one can know I'm hurting

especially            me


I'm out

of tricks


                 delusions     shattered


What are you trying to teach me?

 Can this go any faster?

I fucking hate him in ways that once felt unimaginable.

I hate myself more and I don't know why.

December 30, 2008

Senior year of high school

I don't know why my dad can't stand me right now. I can tell he is trying not to, mostly because mom tells him to be nice. He picks fights with me all the time about stupid stuff like I don't know why. I think it's because I don't compare in his eyes to Keegan and Ryan. I'm sorry I'm not like your precious first born who happens to be perfect and I'm sorry I'm not your golden boy son but even if I was as good a student as Keegan or the athlete Ryan is he wouldn't care anyway because it's already been done so it doesn't matter really how hard I work.

I'm sorry if I'm not quite what I was suppose to be because senior year is kind of "evaluation time" of the person you've become but I don't understand why he wouldn't like me. I've never ever gotten in trouble for anything. I don't know how else I'm supposed to show him... I have stopped wanting to to be honest. I drank Saturday because I was pissed at both my parents like it makes me so mad. Like it makes me not want to tell them the truth. I'm sorry I'm not Keegan and with Ryan it's the "boys will be boys" concept—go ahead and come home at 4 a.m., you're untouchable.

I hate it.

# Tab

**My sister**

*Level 10 Gymnast*

*High School Valedictorian*

*Volunteered at a Children's Hospital*

*State All Around 2003*

*Oregon State Gymnast*
   *(a nationally competitive program)*

*Columbia University Physical Therapy School*

*Big Award from Columbia*

*USC Residency Program*

*Never had a B in her life*

*Beautiful*

*Tiny*

*Adorable*

*Curfew: didn't need it, was always studying*

**My brother**

*Oregon High School Player of the Year*

*Member of the "God Squad" at school*

*100 Meter School Record Holder*

*Nickname is Ferrari...he's fast*

*High School Valedictorian*

*Oregon State University soccer player*

*University of Chicago transfer*
   *(because he needed a more rigorous school)*

*Captain of UC soccer team*

*Shrine of trophies + awards in parents' house*

*Never had a B in his life*

*Curfew: none*

**Me**

*1st Team All State*

*Lost League Player of the Year award by 1 point*

*In and out of the starting line up for my club team*

*3.8 GPA (not a valedictorian)*

*Voted Best All Around of high school class (very palatable)*

*Boise State Soccer team*
   *(left because I was miserable)*

*University of Oregon soccer team*

*I think I got Most Improved one year*

*Masters degree in teaching*

*(Eventually) Professional soccer player*

*Definitely had Bs, and even a C*

*Curfew: Midnight, make sure you wake up mom and tell her you're home.*

*1998*

*At a soccer game of 4th graders. I am in 2nd grade.*

**Coach**: I just really worry about her size, are you sure she should play?

**Me**: *Scores 3 goals.*

*2002*

**Me:** I don't think I want to play soccer next year.

**Dad:** *Blows up.*

*2006*

*My brother's friend making an (astute) observation about my parents.*

**Daniel:** Your dad turned you into killer athletes, your mom made you actual people.

*2007*

**Me:** You know you guys live vicariously through your kids right?

**Mom** + **Dad** : uhhh, duh.

*2009*

**Me**: I don't think I want to go to Boise State and play soccer, I want to go to art school and get into costume design.

**My parents**: Get your degree then you can do whatever you want.

*2009*

*Leaving Boise State because I am miserable and cry a lot.*

**Dad**: I just don't think you should transfer to a PAC-10 school... I worry about your size.

*2013*

*Just graduated from the University of Oregon*

**Me**: I just don't know what I want to do now, there aren't any jobs I really want and I'm not qualified anyway...

**Dad**: You're going to be a teacher and a coach, so just get on with it.

**Me:** *Becomes a teacher and a coach.*

*2015*

**Me**: I'm going to try out for the Thorns, the women's pro team.

**Dad**: Why? You already have a job.

*November 2019, Thanksgiving weekend. Just filed for divorce.*

**Me**: In bed, miserable from my life falling apart, listening to the conversation in the living room.

**Dad**: Do you know how proud my mom would have been to have two grandchildren attend University of Chicago and Columbia?

**Me**: *Rolls over in bed.*

*Sometime starting around 1953*

A husband returns from WWII with PTSD.

Jessie gives birth to my father.

He is the youngest of three boys.

His father leaves the family.

My father grows up without a father.

Jessie remarries and has 3 more babies.

My father's stepfather gets cancer and dies.

My father grows up with five siblings and one mother in a small house.

She raises 6 children on her own.

Her body endures 6 C-sections.

A tornado destroys their house. They live in a mobile home for 3 months.

My dad is in the state championship for basketball. He tells his mother not to come to his games.

My dad loves basketball. He still wishes he would have played in college.

Jessie is a recovering alcoholic.

Jessie dies having only met my older sister.

She is a warrior, one that was forged in the fire.


If she were here to talk, she would understand this far better than me.

It took me a long time to understand why my dad put on suits everyday and drove in traffic to a job he didn't love. He wanted to be a teacher and a coach. He worked in the steel industry for 30 years.

He made enough money to pay for all of his children's elite sports and to send all of them to college without a penny of debt.

My dad grew up without a father.

He worked his whole life to show up for us in ways he was never given; to give us the privilege of a father we could depend on.


His love is my inheritance.

That scene from *Grease* keeps playin in my head. The one where Danny sees Sandy for the first time after the pep rally and Danny blows it because he's trying to look cool in front of his friends. Sandy runs off and Frenchie consoles her, telling her men are rats. She also tells her the only man a girl can depend on his her daddy.

It's complicated, and thank god I had him.

# Tab

Cars given to me by my father .......................................................... 3

Degrees paid for by my father .......................................................... 2

Soccer tournaments paid for by my father ................................... 83

Private trainings paid for by my father ........................................ 730

Trips to Iceland, Hawaii, Mexico, Vegas, San Diego, Seattle, Denver, Sacramento, Tampa, Ecuador......................................a lot.

Times he helped me move out of the dorms .................................. 3

Times he helped me move into the dorms ..................................... 2

Times he helped me move my shit after a break up ...................... 1

Times he paid for my wedding ........................................................ 1

Times he helped me move into a house
I bought and my husband didn't show up ..................................... 1

Times he and my brother helped me coach when I was struggling with divorce ................................................................................... 48

Times he told me I could be anything I wanted to be .................. All the time

Times I watched him be anything he wanted to be .......................
........................................................................................................

Waiting

Everyone is broken and doing the best they can.

May 20, 2018

Year four of teaching

*"An unhappy teacher isn't good for anyone."*

*I'm just trying to make it through the day without losing my mind.*

*I told a girl to shut up last week. In front of the whole class. I apologized right there but Jesus.*

*These kids have so much trauma—dad's in jail, mom's an addict, they were molested by a step parent, they don't have food at the house, they just eat sugar pancakes from the school and takis at lunch...*

*And the district wants us to TEST THE FUCK OUT OF THEM.*

*Like 2 months of classroom time dedicated to test the kids on subjects they don't understand, then they blow up because they feel like idiots because they're hardly there. They're not fed properly. What are we doing here??*

*Even at the high school, I felt like I was taking crazy pills. We had 48 kids on suicide watch. 48. And we were still pushing them to ACHEVE ACHIEVE ACHIEVE. And these were the wealthy kids.*

*No one is actually putting attention and resources to these kids' health.*

*I just can't shake the weight of this world's brokenness every day.*

*May 30, 2018*

End of fourth year teaching

*I'm leaving teaching. Just a break. Just for now. I'll be back. I cannot abandon these kids. But I have to take care of myself for a minute.*

*My mom taught special education for 35 years... I have no clue how she did it. Probably because she's a goddamn saint.*

*I didn't realize how much teaching was chosen for me, between my dad's words and my mom being a teacher, but even my grandmother was a librarian, and her mother was a teacher, and hers too.... Who am I when I am left to my own devices?*

*Who am I when I actually make my own decisions?*

**New boss:** You know, you don't have to spend your life in the trenches.

**Me:** It is the only way I know how to be worthy....

*Dear Maureen,*

*You've been through the wringer this year and have had to put a lot of things to rest.*

*You have been married, a home owner, a teacher, and all are noble pursuits and it took guts to say, "This isn't it."*

*I want you to feel proud of trying and feel no attachment to the feeling that this "should be."*

*You don't have to be anything. In fact, you are just enough as you are. You are allowed to detach, you are allowed to heal your still-fresh wounds. Don't continue to drop acid into them.*

*You can see clearly now. Don't let go of your grounding and always keep your footing.*

*Stay humble and gracious.*

You are a warrior.

You come from a family of survivors.

## Someday

Someday soon

the truth

that only love is real

will thunder through me

Until then

I'll withstand the

pain

of birthing my new life

## Tab

Phone calls with my mom ................. 108

Letters from my sister ...................... 18

Phone calls with Carolynne................159

February 15, 2020

*I can't concentrate. There is so much on my mind. There has been a knot in my chest for a week now and I can't figure it out. I'm tired of being sad. I feel like I'm trying to hold it all together—the sadness, the worry, the stress, not wanting to make the same mistakes. I want to move on though. I've spent SO MUCH TIME BEING SAD. I think part of it is my codependency is just still so active, so if I let myself feel for people I'll just fall back in the trap. I'm so afraid of letting go and just feeling because I don't have control and won't be able to keep the life that is for me.*

*Maybe it is just helpful to admit that what I experienced was actual trauma and I need to also heal from hurt, pain, the damage that was done.*

*To try to hurry up and move on is not going to make it go any quicker.*

As the story goes, the Ship of Theseus was preserved in Athens after a journey from Crete. After some time, the wood started decaying and they had to decide to replace it to maintain the integrity of the ship.

The dilemma is, if you replace the old, original wood with new wood, is it still the Ship of Theseus?

Or is it a new ship entirely?

February 15th, 2020

*You may never get closure.*

*You are meant for so much more.*

*God's plan is bigger than anything you can imagine.*

*Do the right things. Suffering is temporary.*

*God won't give you what you can't handle.*

*You can't manipulate your way from pain.*

*Whatever you need will show itself. Go in the direction you think is best and the universe will provide.*

*I am paying attention to what's going on around me and how I'm thinking and feeling because I love myself, not out of fear of myself as it once was.*

Need to get out of here. But where?

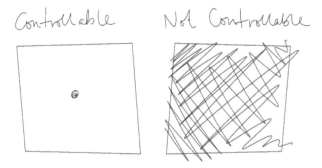

To do : accept the not controllable.

## Since you've been gone

I can finally

breathe

now that you're gone

long enough

to exhale the poison

I can start to see

the skyline of me

through the dissipating smog

When you look back what do you think of?

Thick masks

Undetectable masks

# Performance art

Masks are hard
tough
and dense

Masks are the garden
the porch steps
the fence
we'll never know the feeling
of not being tense

Masks we're not born with
but draw through the years
with colored pencils
labeled with synonyms of fear

Masks tell the truth
that everything's a lie
that emotions in life
should be kept a small size

Like sand on the beach
a missing puzzle piece
steam from too much heat
the food between our teeth

Take off the mask
and we'll all retreat
like there's nothing to breathe
we hate this feeling
of truly
being free

February 26, 2020

*I'm upset at people. XXXX for saying, "I knew the whole time but it wasn't my responsibility." To save me from almost dying??? I'm upset at my parents for not loving me and making me feel like a fucking outcast. And my whole family, my brother and dad for being assholes around me and my sister for never being around or ever being vulnerable or asking for what she wants. I'm frustrated at my ex for being such a mess and I'm even upset at his brother for enabling him and BELIEVING it was my fault. I'm frustrated at my friends for constantly canceling everyone—how are we allowed to be flawed and imperfect? I'm not healthy and I'm tired of being unhealthy. I'm tired of constantly hating my body and my choices in life. Could everyone see it except me? Am I an idiot? I just let this happen? I need to get out of here. Escape this fucking place. I'm overwhelmed with stories about my life and who I was to everyone and what they wanted me to be. Who is that little girl? Who is ten-year-old me? She just wants to be loved. She just wants to be safe.*

February 27, 2020

*Works in progress—that's what we are. Feeling grateful that God has placed the right people in my life. Carolynne has been a guardian angel. I'm grateful for my dad, brother, and Martha for coaching with me, these kids we have around us. After practice I often find myself wishing I could be out of the city more. The stars are so beautiful, it's calm, and there aren't sounds of traffic and people everywhere.*

*This year is going by slow and fast at the same time.*

"Love takes off the mask we fear we can't live without and we know we can't live within."

- James Baldwin

Grant me the serenity to let go of the things I can't control and the strength to control what I can and the wisdom to know the difference. Perhaps I too have been wearing a mask this whole time. The mask of who I thought everyone wanted me to be...

Be kind to yourself, Maureen. You've been through a lot.

Grateful for:

My job that I can call in sick

A nice apartment

My mom picked up the phone

My brother helped me with the dog today

Doggo is healthy

I live in a safe part of the world

I have food to eat

A warm bed

Air in my lungs

What are your anchors? And what are your engines?

What are you worshipping that is causing you suffering?

May 7, 2020

*Just read* This Naked Mind *by Annie Grace...*

*You've been dulling your brain for 10 years now. Alcohol weakens your instincts. Your body is designed to heal you. I've been consuming a drug that has been hurting my brain and body. What could I accomplish with a sober life? What kind of a soccer player could I have been with a sober brain? I spent so much time drinking in college and on the Thorns. I was out of control. ALL of my relationships have started and were sustained because of alcohol.*

*I am so much stronger than I ever believed myself to be. Sad? Have a drink. Happy? Have a drink. Bored? Have a drink....*

## Say ah

I drink for simple reasons—
the ones that make me human

To
sedate the feeling that no one wants me here
sedate the tight fist in my chest
sedate my small boobs and boundaries

and
I drink to forget those reasons

When I was 10 a police officer came to our school and made us write an essay about how we'll never drink or do drugs and I was terrified.

When I was 16 I wanted to be good for my parents so they'd love me so I didn't drink. But then I watched them get drunk watching Napoleon Dynamite with their friends.

When I was 17 I drank from the shot stored in my friend's disgusting UGG boot in her closet and chased it with Apple Jacks. I have never felt so good.

When I was 18 I drank and I felt like for the first time I could stand in a room of people and not feel like everyone hated me.

When I was 19 I drank because I didn't want to remember the reality occurring around me and how much I hated the path that was chosen for me.

When I was 24 I drank wine, gin, vodka, and tequila in one night after my boyfriend told me he cheated on me.

When I was 27 I got drunk at a casual soccer fundraiser, just like I got drunk at all casual things like dinners, Sunday evenings, Friday afternoons, Settlers of Catan, writing events, the bachelor, brunch, hiking....

When I was 28 my meth-addicted husband told me I had an alcohol problem.

When I was 29 the world went into a global lock down and I didn't have to see anyone so I didn't have to drink anymore to wash away the feeling that everyone hated me.

Quiet

is quite

unbearable for most

but it is the only time

I can feel my voice

### Friends in drunk places

What I thought

was a bridge to love

was merely a

broken     pathway

to

the miscarriage

of intimacy

Alcohol doesn't just numb me from sadness and confusion,

but my joy and intuition as well.

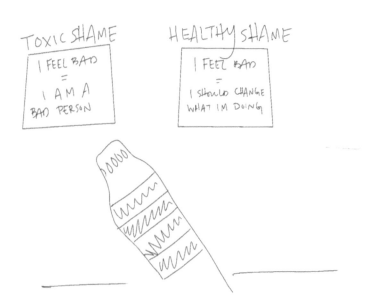

Leaning Tower of Shame

The last time I had a sober first kiss I was 15.

The last time I had a sober first "I love you" was never.

May 23, 2020

*Moment of clarity. Life has to change.*

*I don't know if it was my last business trip in January, I felt so empty, alone, dead inside, even though I was with so many people, staying in nice places, eating good food.*

*Pig Pen—My swirl of dust is definitely too busy all the time with coaching and working. I hardly had a moment to myself this year.*

*Rushing is your response to scarcity. Slow down your thoughts, feelings, emotions. Love is abundant.*

*Souls—definitely feel soulless sometimes.*

*I need to change.*

August 17, 2020

*Feel like my body is getting slimmer which I'm excited about. Adding weights and intermittent fasting has been good.*

*I feel super focused and well.*

*Had an awful dream about my ex last night that I had to fight him off of me and request a restraining order.*

August 18, 2020

*What are my motivations for exercising and eating?*

*My worth is not attached to my appearance.... I don't know how many times I have to say it to KNOW it.*

*I'm still incredibly vain and derive so much self worth from my appearance. I want flawless skin, no fat, to be tan. I'm liking the results of fasting although I don't know how long I can do it for. My motivations are split 50/50.... I want to be fit AND I want to be healthy. It is also okay to be hungry. I'm just used to eating nonstop.*

When I was 4, I sat on a wood bench
after a sunny day of slip and slide
and worried my swimsuit left a mark
showing everyone how fat I was.

When I was 5, I played with
a gorgeous, thin doll
with highlighted blonde hair
and painted nails
and bronzed skin
and a man that loved her.

When I was 11, I was proud of
fitting into the blue Old Navy jeans
I fit in when I was 9.

When I was 14, 15, 16, 17, and 18
I wore make up to school
every single day
and teased my hair
and box dyed it brown
and changed my clothes 4 times
before school
and checked every mirror
to make sure none of the boys knew I was ugly.

When I was 19, I threw up in bathrooms,

binged cookies and drank until I couldn't remember rejection

and hid at home so no one would see

how worthless I was.

When I was 25, I found the courage

to take off my make up for my classroom of 11 year olds,

who told me I looked the same.

When I was 27, I ate very little

and worked out twice a day

and highlighted my hair blonde

and painted my nails

and tanned my skin bronze

so that when I walked down the aisle

I would show everyone

how lovable I was.

When I was 29, I wrote notes to myself

and to my body

to be grateful and to love it

and posted them on all my mirrors.

and sometimes I'd scoff

and sometimes I'd believe it.

## Venting

Maybe I would have

loved myself more

if my toys didn't come with

double Ds and dime-sized waists

Maybe I would have chosen better men

if I wasn't taught I was wrong

and that femininity is the constant pursuit

of self correcting

Someone

somewhere

who I don't fucking know

pays their mortgage with my self hatred

## Tab

1 nutritionist ............................................. $850

10 physical therapist appointments ........ $500

18 therapy appointments .......................... $5040

1 facial ........................................................ $199

12 manicures .............................................. $360

1 energy healer .......................................... $455

2 codependency workshops ..................... $750

1 new wardrobe ......................................... $5638

Makeup, haircare, skin care .................... $1389

September 1, 2020

*I am incredibly judgmental of myself. I need to change my inner dialogue around my body and my thoughts. There is still work I need to do with my therapist on my body, alcohol, clothes, male attention... I think they're all interrelated...*

*1965*

My mother at home after school

**My mother:** Mom, the kids at school are teasing me because I'm so short, they keep calling me shrimp and it hurts my feelings.

**My grandmother**: Just be happy you're not fat.

**Nutritionist:** Your body has been through a lot with college and professional sports and now divorce....

**Me:** I just feel like I'm always working against my body.

**Nutritionist:** You probably don't need to be working out as intensely as you are. More walks, more yoga. Let your body reset and rest.

**Me:** Thank you.

# Tab

University of Oregon Women's Soccer Team

2010-2013

| | |
|---|---|
| Afternoon practice | 2 hours, 4 days a week |
| Night games | 4 hours, 2 days a week |
| 6 a.m. lifting | 1 hour, 3 days a week |
| Times I cried and wanted to quit | 121 |
| Therapy appointments I hid from the coaches | 150 |
| Months without a period | 12 |
| Vodka/tequila/rum shots consumed | Who knows |
| Celiacs disease diagnosis | 1 |
| Hair falling out in clumps | 3 months |
| Cystic breakouts all over my body | 6 months |
| Accutane | 5 months |
| Bronchitis | 2 weeks |
| Pneumonia from the bronchitis | 3 weeks |
| Tonsillectomy from chronic illness | 1 month |
| Summers spent at home | 0 |
| Milligrams of prozac a day | 20 |

October 16, 2010

Sophomore year of college

*Miserable.*

*My body is falling apart.*

*And we just keep going.*

*Studying International Studies has opened my eyes to all of the destruction of the world. I thought I wanted to help but it seems like whenever America touches something we exploit and wreak havoc on innocent people. It's all just really fucked up.*

*I've been thinking about killing myself a lot. I don't really see the point of it all. Like why are we working so hard to join the "real world" when it's such a terrible place. Why did I work so hard to be a soccer player when our coaches are just monsters. I hope they get fired, but they never will. No one gives a shit about women's soccer. If the football team was losing and everyone was miserable they'd get a new coach before the season was even over...*

*I know if I killed myself I would devastate my family, and it doesn't really solve anything. If I have to be here, like on Earth, I'm going to just have to make it a better place. I think that's the only way I can reconcile living.*

**Team doctor:** Sometimes this amount of exercise triggers symptoms of depression (implies that it's not depression).

**Me:** The fuck...

Dear body,

You have provided so much for me from the ability to see the world, hug someone tight, run and play soccer, even in an arena of 20,000 people.

Dear body,

You're pretty badass. I'm sorry for torturing you with exercise and poisoning you with alcohol, processed foods, and sugar. I always want to nourish you.

Dear body,

I'm sorry about all the mean things I have said about you. Society taught me to hate you and my family never taught me how to not hate you. In reality you have showed up for me every day. You've been as present as God has and I just haven't seen it. I now see that love fills every inch of me and is thriving full inside of me.

Dear body,

I vow to stop going out of the way to look in the mirror. I vow to listen, not judge.

When I do look at myself, I will say "I love you."

oh this body

whose heart has

climbed

and climbed

to manifest a breath

that I will always forget to love

"When you are real, you can't be ugly, except for people that don't understand."

- The Velveteen Rabbit

## Letter from my sister

*Maureen,*

*Just a friendly reminder to let you know that I love you and that you are wonderful! I hope you have a week where you feel like yourself, get what you need, and if you're having a rough patch, you at least know that nothing can dim the light that shines from within and that light always shines without you trying. You are heroic, beautiful, kind, strong, vulnerable, and a wonderful sister.*

*I love you! Always!*

*Keegs*

**Affirmations**

My body deserves love and respect.

I love my body as it is today.

I thank you body for serving me today, you always take such good care of me.

Body, I promise to love and cherish you always.

Making myself small does not make me lovable.


I'm sorry for being cruel to you and ask for your forgiveness.

*What I wish someone would have said to me when I was 15.*

You are going through a really tough time right now. You've left middle school and your friends have abandoned you, you switched soccer teams, and you're not getting much playing time and you don't really feel like you fit in with the girls. You're dating an asshole and your best friend doesn't talk to you anymore because she used to date that asshole. Your parents didn't give you any guidance on relationships. In fact, you aren't telling them how hard this year is for you because you don't want to somehow prove you are the "dud of the family."

Maureen, you are NOT the dud of the family. You are talented and loved beyond measure. In fact, God has chosen you and really wants a relationship with you. I'm not talking like those Sunset Presbyterian folks—they're bigoted and homophobic, I know.... They don't really understand God and what She is all about. She is love. And She is present. We just have to let ourselves see it.

I'm going to let you in on a little secret: those girls who were once your friends, the ones you don't fit in with anymore, well they aren't very nice. You, Maureen, are so loving and kind, it's no wonder you don't feel like you fit in! Those girls on your soccer team, they love you, you don't need to be shy or anxious. Your coach is a moron and one day you're going to prove everyone wrong and play professional soccer. You won't do it for your parents or them though. You'll do it for you.

I want you to know, Maureen, that the clothes you buy and put on your body are not important. You are loved and accepted by God. The people are broken and lost; fitting in with the broken and lost only diminishes your light and takes energy from what is important.

You are anything but a dud. You are God's Magnum Opus. Believe in God's love and yourself. Take care of your body and learn the lessons it is meant to teach you. Your body will not lie, nor conceal the truth, hurt, or pain. Love that your body is honest.

Above all else, be curious. Be so curious you fall in love with as many different things as you can because it goes by like that. You have some hard times ahead, but some amazing ones as well. Try not to run from the hurt but embrace it with love. Enjoy being curious and you.

How classic it would be to love someone again.


How wild it has been to love me
for the first time.

## Trying

Checking the mirror less

Listening to my body more

Loving myself and appreciating my goodness

Caring less about vanity

Working out to be healthy, not look good

Writing more fiction and poetry

Admitting that I am lovely

Spending more time in nature

Falling in love with everything

August 13, 2020

*In an effort to spend more time in nature, I have decided to come see Oregon's National Park, the one I have somehow never seen despite growing up here.*

*Today, my friend Kelly and I hiked to the cliff point and sat at the top of Crater Lake. There was a warm breeze paired with a high sun.*

*The brochure says that Crater Lake was formed after a volcano violently erupted amassing the land surrounding it with red hot lava and ash. The landscape burned and created a bowl where the volcano once stood. Over time that bowl filled with water to create the most gorgeous, serene, royal blue lake. It is protected on all sides by land and trees. There is no wake in the water. It just sits. It's etherial and surreal.*

*It is the bluest, clearest thing I have ever seen.*

*I find comfort in knowing that destruction can sometimes bring the most wonderful peace.*

September 16, 2020

*My conditioning is so small*
*in comparison to the bright,*
*warm gold beneath it.*

*My conditioning is plastic*
*and when I burn bright enough,*
*it is dissolved by the inner, real me.*

*The one that is God and love.*

*To melt away such fruitless shields,*
*simply believe in the power of you.*

Melt it day by day

# SPIRITUAL TRANSFUSIONS

Luke 6:20-31

You're blessed when you've lost it all

God's kingdom is there for the finding

**For the illusion of what my life was supposed to look like**

If I let go

I'll make room

for what's to come


Give up the familiar

for the uncharted

unknown

feeling

of love

When I was a ten and my family could afford to give me an American Girl doll, I asked for Kit. Her story took place during the Great Depression. Her family was once wealthy, but was hit hard by the broken economy. They lost everything, their status, their neighbors, their schools, their house, their car, and most of their material items.

Maybe I asked for her because she had short blonde hair like me.

Maybe because she had a typewriter like me.

Maybe because she had a pair of overalls like the ones my grandpa told me he had.

Maybe because I was fascinated by what it meant to lose everything and realize you didn't need any of it.

Who and what are you worshipping?

Our fears

are but delusions

we spin into

a fabric of reality

## Learning

How reluctantly I shed

the things that posed as home

but kept me far

far away

from the heaven

that has been waiting

July 13, 2020

*This time last year I was being told to move out. Migraines and vomiting. Lost. Crying. Overwhelmed. Wondering if "this too shall pass." And it did. I'm off to bigger and better things now and just have to remember that God is taking care of me.*

*I would love:*

*A shift in perception*

*A closer relationship with God*

*A heart that receives love*

*A heart that gives love*

*A gut that is strong*

*Lots of gratitude*

"Miracles are both beginnings and endings and so they alter the temporal order. They are always affirmations of rebirth which seems to go back, but really go forward. They undo the past in the present and thus release the future.

Miracles should inspire gratitude, not awe. You should thank God for what you really are. The children of God are holy and the miracle honors their holiness which can be hidden but never really lost."

-Marianne Williamson, *A Return to Love*

**Me, 10 years old**: Do you believe in God?

**My disillusioned Irish Catholic Dad**: Ahhh, The Great Indifferent.

**Me, 10 years old:** What do you mean?

**My disillusioned Irish Catholic Dad**: Well, I believe there's a higher power, but I don't really think he's paying attention to us. I don't think he really cares.

**Me, 10-29 years old**: Right.

What are the wells you've been drinking from?

Which have run dry?

*Personal inventory on why I hated religion*

My high school boyfriend's parents didn't like me because I wasn't a Christian.

His dad ended up having an affair and leaving the family, which was fucked up.

The church I knew didn't let gay people love, which felt really fucked up.

Evangelicals protesting soldier's funerals felt really fucked up.

Vilifying Muslims felt really fucked up.

I got strep throat at church camp when I was 13 and had to go home.

    Conclusion: God doesn't want me here.

We stopped going to church. We started going to "Our Lady of the Soccer Field" as my dad called it... We just worshipped sports instead.

**My disillusioned Irish Catholic dad**: Man's inhumanity to man knows no bounds. More wars have been fought over religion than any other reason.

**My disillusioned Irish Catholic dad**: My grandfather was Jewish and I used to pray for him to get into heaven. Then one day I realized how stupid that was.

Given the choice, I wonder if God would actually endorse religion...

**Me:** I think I want a better relationship with God.

**My therapist:** Really?? Let's pray. Dear Jesus...

**My therapist:** I spent a lot of time searching and looking at different religions and finally I just surrendered to Christianity. I'm not addicted to alcohol anymore, I'm addicted to Jesus.

Why does saying the name Jesus aloud render the same embarrassment as when I played the penis game on the bus in 7th grade...

**Me**: I just don't know what I am supposed to do next.

**My therapist**: All you have to do is spend time with God and Jesus and they'll show you what to do.

How it feels trying to figure out the
whole God thing...

That scene in *Forgetting Sarah Marshall* where Paul Rudd is teaching Jason Segel how to surf and Paul Rudd is fucking with him.

Paul Rudd relentlessly tells Jason Segal to go from laying down on the board to "popping up", but when he does, Paul get's frustrated and says he's doing too much. Jason Segal tries again and Paul Rudd tells him to do less again. Jason tries again. And again. This cycle continues until Jason Segal just lays on the surf board paralyzed because he doesn't know what to do.

# Tab

Bible from my therapist ............................... 1

A Course in Miracles ....................................... 1

"How to talk to God" books .......................... 4

Unitarian churches visited ............................. 1

Christian "inspired" churches visited ............ 1

Christian churches visited ............................. 4

Christian podcast episodes .......................... 19

Questioning what is the truth ....................... Everyday

## Patience

If the trees can carry the cold winter

with tenacious ice and a truant sun,

then we can surely hold out till

our thawing

**Me, 29 years old**: What are your thoughts on God?

**Mom**: I believe God lives in all of us and loves all of us.

**Me, 29 years old**: Stunned.

**Me, 29 years old**: I never knew you believed that. I was always operating under dad's world view that God doesn't care about anyone... this version feels better.

## Deciduous

Her favorite trees

are the winding winter oaks

who shed their last leaves

exposing swirling shadows

twisting in the moonlight

Her favorite trees

are grounded

just like her

holding simple wisdom:

bend like these branches

and you will find the light

My mother has no idea how amazing she is.

She thinks she is cute and nice.

She is a beautiful woman, even when she does not intend to be.

She takes pride in being small. She learned that is how you avoid shame.

She is a fiery force of love that always does what is right. Even when it is hard.

She brightens everything around her. And yet, she will never know how far her light extends.

She flies near the sun because she was born there.


I am my mother.

## The Endless Well

So warm—

silver frost and bitterness cowers

Glowing—

an exotically

gorgeous woman

Her breath—

is that of still forests

Her magic—

echoes within me

So loving—

She coos you into her stream of belonging

On one prodigious night,

there were tears

that watered a woman in pain

as she birthed a raw, gasping life


My mother did it once

for me


She shoulders my pain

as I do it

now—

my self emerging

*1965 rewrite*

My mother at home after school.

**My mother**: Mom, the kids at school are teasing me because I'm so short, they keep calling me shrimp and it hurts my feelings.

**Her mother**: You are made of me. And I am made of love. Your light is so much bigger than anything we can see. Others will try to diminish your light because you, YOU are magic. Never dim your light. Never dim your love. And above all, never make yourself small. You are the lighthouse for the lost and broken. We need you to shine.

### Remembered Dreams

I never had to plant new seeds

just water the ones

I've ignored all along

"Miracles dispel illusions about yourself and puts you in a communion with yourself and God....

It corrects its errors which are merely lacks of love."

- *A Course in Miracles*

Everything fear based is an illusion.
Only love is real.

Relax into your

noblest surrender


The high priestess

watering flowers

that grow wild with freedom


There is liberty in

relinquishing control

to Love


Collect the

crumbled stories,

cemented together

like ornaments --

and dance on them

while you ascend

to being

## God

Do You remember where I was

when I realized for the first time,

all of those moments

I felt so alone

you were there the whole time

waiting for me

to see?


And I cried

And I cried

And I cried

## Magnum Opus

What if

you were here all along

waiting

for me

to walk out

from behind the curtain

and sing?

Why do we believe it is so much better to get something

consciously

than viscerally?

Cinderblocks of doubt

cursing restless arms

shake them

break them

leave them

FLY

fly hard

for dangerous desires await

the               boundless


and

wild

## If/then

You are of the creator

You are a creation

You are creative

**If/then**

You are creative

Your creations are prayer

I would like to

participate

joyfully

in this world

of suffering

and commit to catching

the rising and

        F

         A

          L

           L

       I

        N

         G

sky

washed with pinks

and golds


I promise to honor

the cold drips of a drink

on a parched mouth


I'll remember to take in fully

the music of my aliveness

leave my cozy chair and

crawl into the covers of my uncharted story

**My dad**: No one gets out of this life alive.

**Me**: Then I guess I will love while I can.

## Imperfect Perceptions

They, she him, or whatever I call God.
Universe, Spirit... language is imperfect...

It doesn't really matter if my version is correct.
It doesn't really matter if I can prove that God exists.

Obsession with understanding
steals from visceral knowing.

It won't matter if it's real.

A simple idea
that love courses through us
and all living things
is the truth I am desperate for.

Love.
It is the reality I crave to create.

## How to talk to God

Stop

open your eyes to the sky

so you catch the rain


It's pouring down

with divine intent


to water the trees

and the flowers

and the people

who need cleansing

August 21, 2020

*A girl bought my couch today. Today is the last day of my 1 year lease and I am moving out because the rent is insane.*

*She was moving out of her fiancé's apartment after they split up. She was sweaty and lost and hustling.*

*It was me a year ago.*

*When I went back into the apartment for the very last time and all of the furniture and dishes and pictures were gone, there was one thing left. A scrap of paper with dust all over it that had been hidden under the couch.*

*It read: "What would God have me learn today?"*

*I cried because of the beauty and power of impermanence. Joy may not last forever, but neither does suffering.*

## Nectar

No longer the flower

but also the bee

I am getting good

at nourishing me

## Prayer

In the mist

breathe into your chest

and hush in its darkness

The Earth's wet tendrils

tossed like new pennies

it holds

every heavy wish

Stand still

and catch it

on rosed cheeks

as it calls for your thoughts

to slow

to look down

to rush to your present

"Dwell in the beauty of life. Watch the stars and see yourself running with them."

- Marcus Aurelius, my grandmother's favorite

Maybe I would have

loved myself sooner

had I known I was made from

an enchanted universe

You're blessed when you've lost it all— all of the distractions and false gods you've been taught to worship.

How wonderfully you shine when you are cut off from the well of empty facades and illusions.

    And you realize love has been in you

    this whole time.

## No place like

Home is a place

that exists beyond space

it sings through our bodies

in the theater of grace

# NEWFOUND EFFUSIONS

Meeting you is good

in the ways a walk near the water

or early morning coffee

need no convincing


You hold back the walls and

and collect each word with your eyes

your body lighting up

my once dark cocoon with your

sarcastic soliloquies

and the encore—

a sturdy hand

holding mine softly


You believe me and my stories and

my human capacity for love

scraps of light fall

through tight cracks of scratched wood blinds

your body the intention of the morning light

lavender and our tired breath envelope our bliss

holding us through the night

## Home

You whisper my name

and my toes curl

to hold me down

to the bed

so I don't float away

**Me**: Have you ever been in love?

**Buck**: I don't know. I thought so, but I'm not really sure anymore.

**Buck**: Have you?

**Me:** I wrestle with that question all the time.

January 3, 2020

*I have turned down other dates but something told me this was worth a shot.*

*Probably the chemistry. I've been trying to listen to my body more.*

*Like how my chest tightens around my ex. It makes me scared and I get this heightened sense of fear.*

*I am still trying to wrap my head around things like forgiveness for myself, for him.*

*My ego was coming up just a few minutes ago that I was making a huge mistake by hanging out with Buck—that it's just going to end the exact same way....*

*But Buck's been nothing but emotionally supportive and loving.*

*We seem to have a really easy time together.*

*I find myself future tripping though because he lives in Louisville.*

*There's something so lovely about him and I've enjoyed getting to know him.*

*I have to remember I am not committing to anything.*

*I think we can just continue to build our friendship especially.*

*It'll be good to know if it's just about the sex... which is wonderful.*

*We just connect on so many things.*

*I guess it makes sense. We grew up together, both played soccer, had the same friends. We just never really knew each other.*

*He has an ease to him that relaxes me, just melts me into presence.*

*He's so funny and sweet. He just smiles at me and holds eye contact without even saying anything sometimes.*

*I caught myself fantasizing while I was cooking and he was fixing the couch in my apartment...*

It is your divine right to be present with love coursing through your soul.

**Buck**: Your capacity for love knows no bounds.

**Me**: Your predictability makes me creamy.

**Buck**: Call that steady or consistent.

**Buck:** Centered.

**Buck**: What motivates you to be a truth seeker?

**Me:** I think it should be the right truths, like fairness, justice, knowing the depths of humanity. Maybe specifically your own humanity.

When I get to see you

and cross your path

in a physical way

with my body

I'll curl into you

inviting your touch

that fills my emptiness

and skin that melts

into plumped lips

a hand that reaches for

more

for deeper

for handfuls of flesh

faces drawn together

stopping to smell the

scent of heat—

the moon and her stars applauding

# Flexible

Your love stretches me

out of my comfortable

loneliness

January 7, 2020

*Where do I begin.*

*My therapist thinks its my codependency that's still really activated which is attracting me to Buck.*

*Which it probably is, but I didn't want to hear that.*

*My time with him was amazing honestly. I felt like we really got each other and I was trying to see him through "Would this be a good partner?" eyes.*

*I got a bit emotional though when the idea of being exclusive came up and Buck said that he didn't think he could.*

*Idk, I'm an idiot and rush into things because I like security but maybe it's also because he said this was the best week of his life and he's never felt this way before and he wants to have my babies and build a house together.*

*His mom said I was her Christmas miracle.*

*He even opened up about stuff with his parents to me and finally talked to them about things that have bothering him for a long time.*

*He said I was his muse.*

*The funny thing is, I am not sure I want to jump into anything either but I still wanted the validation.*

*It's obvious that we have similar values, but there is still a lot of filling of our own cups to do... He's only a year further than me in his own divorce.*

*I get caught up in the security aspect of the relationship and want to rush and that ends up burning me.*

*It's really good he lives 2,000 miles away because Buck said he wasn't ready for a relationship and I KNOW I'm not.*

*It's only the perfect test from the universe to let go and trust the process by being present with myself.*

*You can't force people into too much pressure too soon.*

## Reminder

You will hurt me

because

this is not just my story

of struggles setbacks and redemption

to know

I'm lovable

*it's yours too*

Being present is just paying attention.

<u>Pay attention, Maureen.</u>

You didn't pay attention last time.

## What I want in a partner

Loyal + committed

Hard working

Funny

Emotionally healthy

Desires personal grown and works for it

Takes feedback

Honesty + integrity

Can talk about weird shit

Independent

Caring

Adventurous

Peaceful

Empathetic

Smart

The ego would love to have you unhappy and small, but thats not in your blood.

You are going to continue searching for truth and love.

Love for life, people, places, things.

Fall in love with as many things as you can.

Friendship and release are the foundation of love.

**Healthy boundaries with Buck:**

Keep the good in and the bad out.

Prioritize my emotional and physical health.

Keep my personal commitment to friends and family—don't lose them again!

Go to bed at a decent time. Don't just stay up to talk.

I am responsible for myself and only me emotionally and financially.

I am not his or anyone's emotional crutch.

Be honest about when you're feeling uncomfortable.

Don't do anything you don't want to do.

Respect his wishes to explore his life.

Don't force him into something he's not.

Be supportive as long as it feels okay to you.

Don't give advice unless asked.

I don't have to fix anything.

January 8, 2020

*Victories of today:*

*Brought in new business at work*

*Emailed a mentor because I am NOT a burden*

*Talked to my best friend Carolynne for two hours*

*Prayed for a miracle to end my shopping addiction and to get a hold of my finances*

*Was not worried what people thought of me*

*Thought about growing a side project*

*Buck said he misses me and thinks about me a lot*

January 12, 2020

I booked a ticket to see Buck next weekend. Attention is NOT intention. I just get so excited. I need to slow down. I feel like a fucking idiot.

Dear Maureen,

It's okay. I know you're afraid he'll forget about you and you'll never feel love but if you are meant to be then you have to trust Spirit to guide you and for this to be done the right way. You're panicking about doing this wrong because this feels similar to the old you. You don't have to operate out of scarcity anymore. Love is abundant and you are already filled with it.

January 13, 2020

*Spoke to Buck last night and told him I'm not coming. Of course he was supportive and said to listen to myself and my body. He changed his tune on commitment though. He said he's been thinking about me a lot and thinks we could make it work...*

*We came up with this jar metaphor. I have my jar of marbles and he has his. I know the jar I want, which is a committed, intimate relationship and I am going to be choosy about who puts marbles in my jar and whose jar I put marbles in.*

*I felt like he was deciding which jar to hold, the "intimacy jar" or the "just friends jar." He thinks he wants the intimacy jar and that he wants to put marbles in my jar slowly... mmm*

*There is definitely a part of me that is still mourning so maybe rushing out there to visit isn't a great idea.*

*I pray for slow thoughts and actions.*

*I pray to be guided by Spirit and to listen and trust my inner voice and bring me to safety and love.*

January 16, 2020

On the plane to Louisville.

I've had an array of emotions today.

I think I am on an assignment, truly.

I started to think about my best friend and I didn't want to disappoint her by going because she's been so supportive of me while I figured all this out.

I felt the same level of shame when I thought about my family and friends and how I didn't want to hurt them again.

I feel this pressure for perfectionism now because I feel so royally fucked up.

Maybe I need to be kinder to myself. That I'm allowed to date and figure things out. In fact, it's healthy.

You're not moving there. You're just seeing what it's like and then you can decide if it's realistic or not.

**Friend:** I don't think you should go.

**Other friends**: You should be dating around now and going on lots of dates.

**Carolynne:** Just make sure you're going for the right reasons. Attention is not intention.

**Conversations I made up in my head that my friends were having about me that I cannot confirm**: She's such a fucking mess. She chose a meth addict to marry. She can't make good decisions for herself. Look at her now, flying across the country for a divorced dad. Disaster.

*But a profound leap of faith can be a profound leap of pain.*

*I don't want to leap for men like I did before.*

*I realize now where I've gone wrong. I never believed I had anything worth protecting.*

*I didn't love myself so when I saw my ex's "passion and ambition" for serving others I found it far more important than my own life.*

*I wasn't passionate about anything because passion comes from love.*

*I even think my social justice work may have been driven by ego. I was going to prove my worth and goodness to everyone because I talked about hard topics. But that drip of validation ran dry quickly.*

*That's why I'm not worried about this trip.*

*Maybe my friends are worried. Yes I like Buck but I also LOVE my life and have good momentum and worked myself out of a pit of despair.*

*I am NEVER going back there.*

*I deserve to be loved on and have fun, as does Buck.*

*I don't have plans or an agenda for the future other than simply enjoying this weekend…*

January 20, 2020

*We left things saying we're both committed to seeing this work and see if it will work.*

*The first day I got there I actually got emotional. I could sense how lonely and isolated he was.*

*He was 2,000 miles away from his family and friends. He'd been that way since he had a kid at 20. His childhood was over. His girlfriend was on birth control. They broke up and then she called and told him she was pregnant. I don't know what I would have done if I were her. I don't want to make her into a villain. Going through a marriage, raising two kids, and divorce all completely away from your family... I don't know how he did it. I think the thing that impresses me and scares me the most is that he bet the whole house on himself... literally.*

*He quit his high-paying, toxic job, sold his house, and started his own business. I don't know if I could realistically reject that kind of security with the belief that I could simply, "do anything."*

*Obviously the situation has its issues but it feels like one where two people have done, and are doing the work.*

*First night we ran into each other. Drunk.*

**Me**: What did you learn from your divorce?

**Buck**:

**Buck**: That I can do anything.

I'm starting to believe that if I spent even a fraction of the effort I spent trying to make my marriage work on ANYTHING else in my life, I would be a fucking star.

*Remember when you called me right before my birthday and wouldn't sign the papers.*

**Ex:** I don't understand what you want.

**Me:** I want you to sign the divorce papers. This is not a game. I don't want anything from you. I truly believe our relationship is toxic and we both need to move on to heal.

**Ex:** I've written a suicide note... I also never forgave you for telling my mother I left rehab to keep using...

**Me:** Did you want an answer from me or to just tell me about it?

**Ex:** Just tell you about it.

February 4, 2020

*Take what works, leave the rest.*

*Put yourself in a house where truth is told.*
*Go out on the roof, see all the fires and stay there.*
*Until you are carried to the peak of a mountain.*
*Live there until you become a house of your own.*

*You can push off from here. You don't have to feel this way again.*
*The time is near to come forward with whatever killed your spark.*
*There's no such thing as the future when the past has you by the throat.*
*How bold one gets when one is so sure of being loved.*

**Buck**: Maybe when you get back to your oasis instead of going back to help others find it, your light helps brighten up the oasis for others who are on the edge and searching for it.

We are the light house, not the boat.

We risk drowning if we go back into the current.

February 15, 2020

*I'm so afraid I'll drop everything and move to Kentucky to "fix" this person, like I'll fall into a role like before.*

*He said he is falling in love with me and has never felt this way before. But he also is retreating a bit...*

*I'm so afraid of letting go and just feeling because I won't have control and won't be able to keep the life that is for me.*

**Text message from ex:** *Pictures of you. Just pictures.*

## Affirmations

I am loved.

I am loving.

God, please point my feet in the direction to joy and passion.

Please guard and place my heart in the hands of those who will cherish it and protect it.

March 24, 2020

*Quarantine—day who knows.*

*Today is the first day I've been hit with loneliness. I don't even really know what I crave but maybe it's that I haven't talked to God today.*

## Tab

Texts with Buck ................................................... 1,085

Hours on FaceTime with Buck ............................ 84

Days spent in person with Buck .......................... 24

Sober "I love you" for the first time ...................... 1

Months waited for ex to sign divorce papers ...... 5

June 20, 2020

*Finally back in Kentucky.*

*Lot's of kayaking, runs, soccer.*

*We spent time on the lake with the kids and his aunt and uncle.*

*After, we went back to their farm.*

*The sun was setting and the air held it while Buck and I sat on a swing tied to a tree.*

*It was gorgeous.*

*I didn't want it to end.*

## Our Song

The soft wind whistles a tune

of redemption for our

sanguine hearts

The trees bristle with applause

and the grass sways with

summer's slow dance

I'll move with you

as long as it's always this way

This summer evening is

filled with a sky that crawls

to the river


White clouds cradle

a rose and blue canvas melting

into a

**slow motion melody**

July 4, 2020

*Buck is here in Portland.*

*I really liked it when I visited Louisville actually.*

*The hard part is I feel hesitant... I don't want to to abandon my family.*

*I really do love Buck and spending time with him.*

*Kids are a lot to consider too... I just have a lot on my mind.*

## Checks + balances

I could watch you all day

the way you breathe in

between your teeth

and exhale the galaxy

Your bare feet dragging across

the floor like a slow burn

I'll pretend I'm not

watching you

I'll even seem distracted

But really

I won't let myself

enjoy you

fully

in case you ever leave

July 5, 2020

*Buck told me I was the love of his life. It scared me to hear that honestly...*

*My ex said that and continues to say the same thing.*

*Did I believe he was the love of my life or did I just go with what he was saying?*

*Is it deep down I don't feel lovable?*

*I'm still very much in a "season of me" and feel the messy residue from last year.*

*I don't want to hurt Buck by taking it slow for myself but I have to for my healing.*

July 8, 2020

Buck went back to Kentucky today. I'm torn because I miss him and I know that I still need a lot of time to process and heal.

I guess I'm confused by everything.

Like why my ex? Why did I get married?

Why Buck and Kentucky? Why his ex?

If he was there this whole time why couldn't we have just been friends or together when we were kids and avoided all this pain?

Why couldn't Buck have come home from school that summer she got pregnant?

Why couldn't we have just started dating after college, got married, bought a house, played catch in the front yard and had a life of happiness?

But I guess that would have made us predictable?

I had momentum towards divorce and healing this year and now the divorce is final. I just feel really stagnant, like I don't know what to do next.

Buck was really sweet and supportive about me feeling really lost, really encouraging to everything I said, and wants me to be whatever I want.

I'm just haunted by the ghost of my ex. I need it to leave.

"Blessed are the forgetful, for they get the better even of their blunders.

How happy is the blameless vestal's lot! The world forgetting, by the world forgot. Eternal sunshine of the spotless mind! Each pray'r accepted, and each wish resign'd."

-Frederich Nietzsche

July 19, 2020

*You have permission to take your time, especially with Buck.*

*We had a really nice conversation this morning where he told me that he feels he could see us being really good for each other long term.*

*He wants to be with me and has never felt this way before and feels that this is it for him.*

*I'm still working on learning to accept love for myself and love from him.*

*I am subconsciously waiting for him to back out or for the red flags to appear.*

*I have transformed so much in a year. What if I keep changing and Buck doesn't feel the same way about me?*

July 27, 2020

*I'm feeling really conflicted.*

*Buck and I broke up and it's because I'm dead inside.*

*I don't know how to receive love. I feel numb to a lot.*

*At first I was frustrated that I'm not "further along" but I feel like he's a lot more ready to give to the relationship than I am. I feel guilty being with someone where I don't know the plan, or my plan I guess.*

*I don't want to leave Portland any time soon and maybe I just still have a lot of shit to sort through.*

*It's a lot of pressure on me to be the one to move because he can't with kids and his ex and I'm scared.*

When someone tells you they love you

you don't have to run

you don't have to hide

or build a wall

when someone gives you

that thing you've been searching for

you know you can take it

cradle it in your hands

and hold it close to yours

when they look at you

and catch your eyes with steady beats

you can keep looking too.

Dear ex,

I asked you to not contact me. But you did. "You and Migos are missed."

Fuck you. You're the reason my world fell apart. You're the reason I'm in debt. You're the reason my heart is broken and I feel nothing. You're the reason I can't love fully. You're the reason I can't believe anyone would love me.

If I can't accept God's love, how could I ever accept human love?

**To do:**

Think less. Feel more.

Find a source of unconditional love.

I am loved even (and especially) when I stumble.

**Stop:**

being overly nice

people pleasing

over/under eating

fantasizing

seeking revenge/justice

ruminating

saving others

changing careers

moving constantly

headaches

tight chest

hip pain

July 28, 2020

Evening

Would have been 2 year wedding anniversary

*Big day today. I asked for a miracle and I think I got one.*

*God has been here this whole time. I can now see God. He is present because he always been been. I was just clouded by lies about him.*

*I chucked my wedding ring in the Willamette River. I asked God to rid me of my pain and burden of my sins and former self. Rid me of the pain of marriage so I could move on and join the universe and listen to it and be what it has in mind which is to be unconditionally loved. I saw myself in all of those hard moments where I felt alone and unlovable and God was there. He was watching this whole time.*

*I feel like I closed a major book today and I get to start a new one tomorrow. A new sequel that has already been written. I just have to follow the plan...*

*It is not up to me to uncover the light in others. Only to find the light already within me. Only then will I share the light of God.*

August 1, 2020

*When you are afraid of anything you acknowledge the power to hurt you.*

*I told Buck everything I was feeling and that I love him.*

*He is right in not wanting to get too excited.*

*I don't want to get hurt again.*

*He's been a champion and support system for me.*

*Just cut him some slack and let him live his life.*

"It is through love all pain turns to medicine."

- Rumi

## Cocoon

when I told you I had never
really had a best friend and I
started tearing up a bit –

you enveloped me and held me
tight and warm.

you told me you'd be my best
friend.

and I just cried endlessly, like I
couldn't stop because I could
finally feel your love.

                    wrap your arms and legs

                                        around me


                    twist and
        turn like
                        roots of
                    my favorite
            oak
                            tree

What if we were just two flowers that thought they were strange in just the right way

we were just two flowers that had to endure a long and cold December

we were just two flowers that knew to hold out for the warmth we'd only imagined

we were just two flowers that had to grow

enough to see each other

we were just

September 29, 2020

*On the plane home from Louisville.*

*It was a really lovely time. It was easier this trip.*

*I'm a lot more healed and so is he.*

*We honestly just had fun... such a strange concept.*

*Buck said when I was leaving that he's never felt this kind of love before, that he feels like he's in high school again.*

*I have to agree.*

*I've never been in a relationship where the other person was my true best friend.*

*The word "best friend" was certainly thrown around in past relationships but it wasn't really friendship.*

*I feel like I'm seeing him differently now. Like I'm not evaluating him to be perfect but appreciate his humanness.*

*Two individual people with full cups who compliment each other immensely.*

*He does a lot and is driven and ambitious and a really good dad.*

*Buck has poured so much love, laughter, and joy into my life when I needed it the most.*

*There are still things I'm working on, and him too, but if we feel this good 9 months into a slow burn, it's just going to get better.*

## This is intimacy

Your hands feel like
 the twilight wind

I didn't know I needed them
until they caressed my face
and showed me how
to hear the light

March 12, 2020

*This virus, it's worse than I thought.*

March 13, 2020

*A woman was sleeping in her bed in Louisville, Kentucky. She was shot and killed in front of her boyfriend who was soon to propose. They probably said goodnight and kissed each other and fell asleep under warm covers after a long day.*

*Breonna Taylor was murdered by Jonathan Mattingly, Brett Hankison, and Myles Cosgrove.*

"And one time my dad said to Breonna, What do you want to sing? And she said, I want to sing Johnnie Taylor, 'Last Two Dollars.' Everybody just fell out, like where did this little girl come from? And everyone was like, I got to see this. And they put this song on and gave her the mic and she was just going at it. And I was like, Oh my God! Everybody loved Breonna. Who wouldn't love a baby? But literally she was everybody's baby.... "


- Ta-nehisi, Coates, "THE LIFE BREONNA TAYLOR LIVED, IN THE WORDS OF HER MOTHER"

June 15, 2020

About to go to Louisville

My family is really worried about my upcoming trip to Louisville. They think it's a war zone. There's been so much news lately about the "riots." Another man, David McAtee was shot by the police...

Buck says it's okay in his part of town.

I told my parents that there is plenty in the news about Portland and they don't seem too concerned about that.

I'll be good, I tell them.

It's not like Portland has been better...

Oct 15, 2018

Teaching

No students yesterday at school. I was selected to participate in an active shooter simulation. The SWAT team came to school and there was police tape everywhere and they shot blanks in the hall and we had to run into any classroom we could find and barricade the door and hide.

Then we went home like it was another day at work.

Today, when all the kids were there, back at school, a police officer fired a blank to trigger a simulation drill and all the kids rushed into classrooms and I barricaded my door and I had to tell my crying children that this wasn't real. It was PRACTICE. PRACTICE FOR BEING SHOT BECAUSE WE BELIEVE THAT TO BE A STUDENT IN AMERICA MEANS THE POSSIBILITY OF DYING AT SCHOOL. And no one really cares.

How in the fuck are we paying for the police to come in and shoot us up and we aren't paying for anything remotely close to moving the needle on these kids' mental health? How the fuck are my students who are black, brown, and poor white kids expected to feel safe? Aren't they here to learn? Let's keep reminding them that their life is a war zone.

The fact that 75% of the teachers in America are women should say something. No wonder we shit on them. This system takes advantage of our kindness by paying us nothing, giving us no resources, and then expecting us to handle a psychopath who wants to shoot up a bunch of little kids.

Everyday at this school, we wear whistles around our necks everyday like a gym teacher. If a shooter comes into the school, we're supposed to blow the whistle. Every time I look at this fucking whistle, I wonder if today's the day.

## My body, no choice

I sometimes wonder when

the National Anthem

sings of bombs bursting in air

and the NRA determines

our elections

and our President is

the Commander in Chief

and our police carry assault rifles

and shoot black and brown people

like target practice

and our military spending is

5 times more than we spend on education

and grown white men shoot up schools

and children die

and gun sales go up...

I sometimes wonder

if we even have a choice

## Privilege

is never

having to whisper

to yourself

you are safe

## Teaching Tab

*Number of times...*

A male student asked me to prom ............................................ 3

Male students took pictures of me
without my consent ................................................. 5 (to my knowledge)

A 6'4 male student stopped me in the hall
and wouldn't let me pass ......................................................... 3

A 6'4 male student grabbed my hands in the hall .................... 1

I made sure my ass wasn't too sexy or
I didn't show cleavage ............................................. Every day

I didn't buy something because it
might be too sexy ................................................... All the time

I worried that my body might
be a problem in the classroom ............................... Every day since I was 15

## Faces

A man in a white truck x 4

A man in a black truck x 5

A man in a honda x 3

A man walking x 12

A man on a bike x 3

A stadium of men x 3

A man who grabbed me and kissed me in broad daylight x 1

A man who grabbed my ass while I walked to the bathroom at a bar x 6

A man who thought a dick pic was a nice birthday present x 1

A man who grabbed my ass while I sold raffle tickets x 1

A male friend who grabbed my boobs as a joke x 2

## Places

The Pearl District

Quito, Ecuador

North Portland, Oregon

New York City

My classroom

Beaverton, Oregon

The street I grew up on

Outside the daycare I worked at

Seattle, Washington

Outside Hot Lips Pizza in the rain

Timbers Stadium

Snapchat

Guadalajara, Mexico

## Cat Calls

Any hour

any street

I can hear

the whistle

of a boy

who was taught

that absolving women

of their safety

is what it means to be a man

Name me a time when the male body was up for political discussion. Name me a time we didn't rush to medicate the limp dick. Name me a time we shamed men for deciding parenthood wasn't the right choice. Name me a time a man was too bossy. Name me a time a man's title was defined by his marital status. Name me a time a man had his belly rubbed without asking. Name me a time men had to go to the bathroom in pairs so they wouldn't get raped. Name me a time a man worried if he was taking up too much space. Name me a time a man wasn't insulted for "playing like a girl." Name me a time a man apologized for existing. Name me a time men had to fuck up their hormones to let their partner ejaculate. Name me a time a man was not the president of the United States. Name me a time when a man was worried about walking in the dark. Name me a time a man was held accountable to violence. Name me a time when boys weren't just boys and functioning adults that can control how they move in the world. Name me a time a man was a slut for sleeping around. Name me a time a man wasn't kept alive over a girl when forced to make a choice. Name me a time a man was expected to put out cuz a woman paid for dinner. Name me a time they burned a man for being a witch. Name me a time someone didn't trust a man's opinion because he was a man. Name me a time when a man's choice to family planning was protested outside the clinic. Name me a time a man was asked how he was going to juggle fatherhood and work. Name me a time a man was denied birth control. Name me a time men were asked to go home and bake cookies to be less threatening. Name me a time men were considered property. Name me a time a man was pitied for being single. Name me a time a man was raped because he was asking for it. Name me a time a man was sexy if he was skinny and hungry. Name me a time a man didn't go to school cuz they didn't have money for a tampon. Name me a time a man was described in the bible for their sexual status. Name me a time men were only allowed to be cheerleaders. Name me a time the president bragged about grabbing men by the dick. Name me a time when men were not allowed to attend college. Name a time a man was denied credit unless their wife's name was on it. Name me a time a man was expected to take his wife's last name. Name me a time men weren't allowed to vote. Name me a time men were expected to sleep with their superiors to get ahead. Name me a time a man was more worried about being killed than his date being fat. Name me a time a movement had to be created to stop sexually abusing men. Name me a time when a man's role was in the home. Name me a time a man wasn't fit for office because he had emotions. Name me a time a man was scrutinized for showing nipple. Name me a time when a man dressed up as a woman and it wasn't hilarious. Name me a time a man didn't pee in public. Name me a time a woman orgasmed and the man didn't and that was the norm. Name me a time a man spent their morning plucking, teasing, and waxing because hair was unsightly on them. Name me a time a man thought about the impact of his words on the other people in the room. Name me a time a man was convicted and punished for rape because it didn't matter if it "impacted the life of the athlete." Name me a time we taught boys it was okay to be sad. Name me a time it wasn't dehumanizing to be called a pussy or a bitch. Name me a time we didn't already know all of this.

*My addict husband taking my dog and threatening to drive away:*

**Me** *having never shouted at anyone in my entire life:* Give me back the fucking dog or I will call the fucking cops!

**Him:** Call the cops, that's such a white thing to do!

I know what it looks like, he was right, but I didn't know what else to do.

July 21, 2020

*I can hear helicopters all day and all night. Trump sent in his goon squad-gestapo to Portland. How is this legal? They can't kidnap people for peacefully protesting.*

*The city feels different than it ever has before. It's alive and angry and the protests are never ending... and yet it's still the same sleepy place with soft trees and people gathering on picnic blankets like nothing is wrong... like nothing is wrong.*

September 14, 2020

*The sky is smog.*

*Everyone is told to stay inside.*

*Yesterday I fell asleep at 10 a.m. and slept the entire day.*

*The west coast is on fire.*

*I walked around Forest Park with my brother and I don't have words to explain the devastation of looking out onto the city and seeing nothing.*

*Nothing but smoke.*

*You can't even see the other side of the river from the shore.*

*I don't mean to be dramatic.*

*But honestly, this feels like dooms day.*

*Between covid and the police and the troops and the fires,*

*I don't know this place anymore.*

It crawled forward
slowly
then
all at once

Smoke filled my lungs
took my breath
so I'd listen long enough to hear
the cries for too much

But we'll keep climbing,
succeeding
taking
using the Earth like a woman's body
without consent or care
objectifying it
colonizing it
and qualifying it with
progress

A word synonymous with
destruction
devastation
molestation

Heavy ash and dirtied masks
burning skies falling on dead grass

Draw me a picture of the sky
use blue like we used to

Make it stop
like we made it start

It's exhausting pretending
like this was a fluke
like this year was an accident

Kill.fuck.marry.

patriarchy

white supremacy

capitalism

*The virus, it's worse than we thought.*

*And it just keeps fucking going.*

September 23, 2020

*Back in Louisville for Buck's birthday in a few days.*

*Breonna Taylor's verdict was announced.*

*Brett Hankison was not charged for any crimes related to her death.*

*He was charged with wanton endangerment of her white neighbors.*

*The city has been shut down.*

*All businesses are closed and boarded up. It's 4 p.m.*

*I can feel the city and its pain.*

*The people and the weight of hatred.*

*The weight of genocide.*

*I don't know why we get our hopes up that justice will be served. Like THIS will be the moment where they did the right fucking thing.*

*Breonna died in her bedroom for a crime no one around her committed. Her bedroom.*

*I can't get over the fact that she was sleeping. In her bedroom. And they came in like the gestapo.*

*HOW ARE THEY NOT THE GESTAPO?*

*I can't stop crying. For Breonna, for the city, for the country.*

*I cannot get over the world's cruelty and injustice. She was a good girl and she was murdered anyway.*

*How is everyone not heart broken?*

*Breonna Taylor was murdered by Jonathan Mattingly, Brett Hankison, and Myles Cosgrove.*

*They were not charged with with her murder.*

*They are walking around free.*

      I feel deep in the marrow of my bones,

          the weight of how much America fears black people,

          and how much America hates women.

Breonna was goodness

She sang songs of blues
Her everybody voice
it moved in bodies and
melted frost paned windows

Oh sweet girl, where did you come from?

Old, her soul
too bright
for horrid men
who went home and kissed
their wives after
another day at the office

The world is singing your name

Breonna

If you want
to do a girl a favor
marry your mind to your soul
let her name move in your body
and shout until she runs
through the soil
and echoes
through roots
that give birth to us all

"I think it's a sad thing, and I give my regards to the family of Breonna. I also think it's so sad what is happening with everything about the case—including to law enforcement.

"Praying for the two police officers that were shot tonight in Louisville, Kentucky. The federal government stands behind you and his ready to help."

- 45th President of the United States

## How tyrants are born

The power and glory
of the imagination is a
noble badge of honor
humans can claim

What devastation and decimation
a love starved soul can bring

In place of a heart
there will be nothing
no kindness
no sadness
no empathy
no light

Their imaginations
were never fed
they became greedy
like a lion surviving a drought

So they build a world
that resounds their spirit
dark and broken

Fear their badge of honor

September 29, 2020

*Watching two grown men yell and talk over each other on TV. They're both very old and very white. One was elected after he was caught saying he likes to grab women by the pussy. It wasn't the fact that he said such awful things about frankly everyone that shook me. It was the fact that white women still voted for him.*

*Oh god, white women... We must absolutely hate ourselves.*

For a long time as a white woman

I hated myself.

There is nowhere for you to go.

Not really.

As a woman you worry about your safety and the space you take up.

As a white person you worry about the violence of your whiteness and the space you take from others.

Just be nice was

my conclusion.

Make the world a better place

would be my legacy.

But don't be a white savior.

Leave no trace of your whiteness.

Not even a baby.

The world doesn't need any more white people.

Shrink it. Destroy it. Hate yourself until it disappears.


How do I move in the world to disrupt the terrorism that is my skin color?


How do I ask this question without making it about me?

This whole year, I've asked...

How did I choose to marry such a storm of a person?

But how did an entire country fall for this tragedy of a president?

**Question:** If there was one moment that sort of defined your relationship with this world what would it be?

**Answer** : That's the worst part about it. There was no sweeping moment where I knew it was unhealthy.

Being a woman, it is death by a thousand cuts.

in no place or time

(in my recollection)

has there ever been

one thing

in the entire reality I live in

that was not designed and

ran

by men

## Blueprint

And how

is the moon to shine bright

in a world

created for the sun?

Everyone is broken


and I find it hard to believe people are doing
the best they can.

There is an unwavering exhaustion in the pursuit of *goodness* in a place that doesn't actually give a fuck.

This isn't a fairy tale where benevolence prevails.

"Fairness" is a myth, not a universal truth.

But *power*...

If there are so many things—laws and people and stories and systems—working against us, they must be terrified if that power was ever realized.

I don't want more power in your patriarchy

I want to burn it down

and with its ashes

build utopia

the one they kill people for imagining

There is nothing left to worship here

This place

it's rules

it was all a set up

Keep ourselves small

palatable

in the name of *goodness*

Being a good girl

what a scam

There are still so many stories to unlearn

# OVERWHELMING CONFUSION

October 26, 2020

*Finally made it to Kentucky. It was an extremely long drive and I don't want to think about doing it again.*

*Listened to the book* Sapiens *and honestly the conclusion I have drawn is that all of this is made up.*

*This life, all of this, is just people's imaginations. We should have just stayed hunters and gatherers.*

*Humans are just awful, awful animals. We kill each other, other animals, suck the life out of the Earth, all for some made up bullshit that we all just happen to agree upon.*

*I wondered at times if it was all worth it or if I should have just flown, but driving allows me to bring sweet doggo Migos so we can stay for more than 10 days and see if this is actually "something."*

*Buck dropped everything and met me in Denver and drove 1000 miles back with me.*

*I am excited to see what this new chapter brings, although I already miss home.*

*I am proud of myself for putting myself out there and doing all of this.*

*Am I going above and beyond for love though?*

*It was simpler to do the love thing at a distance... All I know is this is getting real and it's scarier than I thought.*

**Inner Critic:**

You aren't deserving of love and happiness.

Your life is insignificant.

You should feel ashamed of your past.

If you're not in alignment with God, you will definitely make the wrong choice.

The wrong choice is always waiting.

October 30, 2020

*I'm tired and anxious.*

*I feel it in my chest and gut.*

*I am really missing my family.*

*Having drove out here I feel so stuck.*

*I know I just have to sit in my feelings and feel everything to make the best decision.*

*I know that Buck loves me and that I love him but love is not enough. It is about a lot more than that.*

*I'm just trying to figure out if this is really what God has planned for me.*

*Maybe I'm not deserving of another person's love and commitment.*

*Maybe I'm meant to live in solitude and live the rest of my days learning to love myself better because the reality is, you can't really trust anyone.*

*You can always get hurt.*

*Even your family will hurt you immensely.*

*Even the person you thought was your husband will hurt you immensely.*

*I'm just indulging in self loathing…*

*I won't feel this way forever and I know no one knows me better than God and maybe one day I'll have a happy ending.*

**Me**: I'm just so worried that I'm making the same mistakes again. It just feels like nothing is good…

**Friend**: He is not your ex-husband by any means. Your ex was cruel. Buck has a huge heart.

**Me**: I think I'm just so embarrassed to be divorced. Like I made a terrible decision before marrying him and I don't want to make a bad decision again.

**Friend**: You shouldn't be so embarrassed by your divorce. We're all on our own paths and no one is "killing it."

But what is the path?

November 1, 2020

*I am about to go to a cabin two hours away to recenter. I don't want to drive all the way home but I can't make sound decisions for myself while I'm here because I'm afraid my codependency is taking over. I have to have some time to myself to know deep down what I really want. Not what he wants or the kids want. I know that he loves me and last night he told me that I showed him what real love is and that it actually existed.*

*I think it comes down to, "Is this the life that I want?" These aren't my kids and maybe I do want kids of my own with someone. And do I want to raise them away from my family? He was in it before he got to experience his independence. He'll be 45 when his daughter graduates high school. I don't want to lock him down for more time... I see how hard it is to raise kids and I've always been hesitant of it.*

*When I was younger I always said, "I can barely take care of myself—how would I take care of someone else?" Now I'm finally getting good at taking care of myself. Do I want to add on others to take care of too?*

*God, please point my feet and fill my heart with love. Heal my wounds and guide me to my purest self.*

Being in love
feels like a petty gesture
after an obliterated marriage

*Who am I to enjoy this?*

Being in love could mean
pouring acid back into the wounds
I've worked so hard to heal
I'll hold my arms out and keep you far away
to avoid the agony of feeling.
I'll walk through life with armor
and therefore with wisdom

Being in love is like
learning to sing
after a totaled spirit

Who am I to get a second chance?

November 3, 2020

*Election Day. I'm at "grandpa's cabin" and it's lovely here. The windows are big and the trees pour in. Perhaps they have something to teach me.*

*I guess I keep coming back to the fact that my life is better with Buck in it.*

*He helped me so much at my darkest and brought me back to life. I have a lot of questions to really consider though.*

*Do I want my own kids?*

*Do I want to get married again?*

*Do I want a life partner?*

*I lost my entire identity and spirit last time...*

*Is this the reality I want to choose?*

*We've both been married before so we're just afraid and I don't want to force him into a life he didn't chose again.*

Motherhood.

Taking care of another person.

Children that aren't biologically mine.

I didn't get 9 months and a bucket of hormones to attach to them.

I am meeting and getting to know them like any other person.

I fear losing independence.

I fear losing myself in taking care of someone again.

I fear falling into a role.

I fear I'll want my own.

I fear I'll never want my own.

I fear that I will be so consumed in the lives of everyone around me, I will forget who I am and when I'm old and grey I will be tired with regret that I gave it all up for this thing they say you're supposed to want.

Is there something wrong with me?

November 3, 2020

*The world's problems are endless and can overwhelm you. That's part of my hangup with kids:*

*I can't take care of myself—why take care of a kid?*

*The world is broken—why bring a kid in?*

*We're overpopulated as it is.*

*What value do they bring to us as humans?*

*When I was teaching I used to say things like "kids are just down" and they're pure and they haven't been jaded by society yet. It befuddles me that people are having children intentionally right now. Are they ignorant or optimistic? Are we on the brink of destruction or the brink of utopia?*

What stories can you get rid of to

make room for better ones?

Trees have strong, thick trunks

with offshoots and wooden sighs

branches that fight

to catch a glimpse of the sun

stretching longer and weaker

until they cease in mid air


When the air gets crisp and hollow

they'll shed all but their favorites

then they even get rid of those...

Because life is not forever

they know that death means new things to come


If trees measured their worth on salvaged leaves

they'd miss the celebration of roots

that have attached so firmly

beneath the surface

and danced together so freely

the soil doesn't know who is who


They'd miss the pleasure of vulnerable rays

that can only come from saying goodbye to

what no longer serves them


When the moment is right they bloom with delight

like medals

they show off the fruits of enduring a

resurrection and radiate

for all to see

November 4, 2020

I texted Buck last night and he said he misses me so much. I believe we can make it work and I believe we have something special in the relationship. I want to get clear on what I am to his kids. Like what is my role? I'm not their mother... I have to remember, I have never done this before...

Maybe this is just a year of being tested. Fall is about shedding the old, so perhaps we're all meant to decide what to keep and what to get rid of. Like my ideas around family, motherhood, and perfection...

You're not going to avoid pain by being cautious and keeping people at a distance and not committing.

You need to lean into all the human parts of you. The ones you're most ashamed and afraid of.

It's been a hard year of covid, distance, and divorce. Be kind to yourself.

Appreciating:

The sun opening its eyes to the beauty of the scattered leaves.

The forest calm in stillness.

Every once in a while the tree will shed a leaf

but most are gone already,

exposing branches of delicate precision.

November 5, 2020

*Had a pretty big conversation with Carolynne last night. I was spinning in my thoughts and realized just how deeply terrified I am of making the wrong decisions. My 20s are this dark spot of shame for me that I'm hell-bent on proving I'm not a fuck-up.*

*I feel like I'm doing everything I can to protect myself like listening to my body, yoga, journaling, nature, breathing, boundaries, slowing down, not drinking.*

*It seems all healthy and stuff but honestly I'm just white-knuckling it to so my life won't fall apart.*

*Carolynne said God doesn't care if you make mistakes. God is always present.*

*I was thinking so much in the binary that either I am aligned with God or I am not; if I make the right decisions it will prove I am in alignment with him, and if I make the wrong decisions it will prove I haven't really healed at all.*

*But that's just not true. I'm just tired of feeling paralyzed by my past.*

*But what is losing?*

*And what is winning?*

*Maybe losing is doing the same things and expecting different results.*

*Maybe losing is not growing or learning from the lesson the universe assigned to us...*

God point my feet and love me through this wandering journey.

I am trying to figure it out and I know you love me for that.

I promise to never leave a lesson unlearned.

"Abraham was exceptional not because he was pious but because he accepted the preposterousness of his own predicaments."

- Jordan Kisner, *Thin Places*

**Me**: I just think I'd be giving up so much of myself if I came to Louisville permanently.

**Mom**: You wouldn't really be giving anything up. All the work you have done is still inside you. You could be gaining a lot...

**Me**: What is there to gain?

**Mom**: Someone to build a life with.

**Affirmations:**

You are powerful. You are loved.

There are miracles happening all around you.

The world is inherently good—we just have to choose to see it.

Everyone makes mistakes. No one is perfect.

# Time

Surrender

like the flower to the sun

my cold winter is over

but only if I choose

to open to the light

You're allowed to leave the realm of the problem.

**Me**: Is it okay if I come back tomorrow morning?

**Buck**: Absolutely dear. I'd have you right now.

December 9, 2020

*A lot of life has come to me passively by simply pursing an interest and sticking with it. Follow your curiosity down a path of the unknown as far as it can take you.*

*A lot on my mind but no longer ruminating. I've made a plan to drive home to Portland in time for Christmas. I feel like I can relax now.*

*Had a good talk with Buck. We're just not eager to repeat our former lives of house, marriage, kids. I still like living in Portland and desire my independence—although the closer I get to leaving Louisville, the more sad I feel.*

*I had it in my head that I would hurt him by taking it slow, but we realized we can make this relationship anything we want. It doesn't have to look conventional. I didn't know love could be freeing.*

*Wednesday: Omaha*

*Thursday: Cheyenne*

*Friday: Twin Falls*

*Saturday: Portland*

**Affirmations:**

Surrender to the unknown.

Hold off on conclusions.

Stay in the realm of the solution.

December 15, 2020
On the road somewhere between Omaha and Cheyenne

*My dad said he wishes I would have met Buck before my ex-husband. I wish that too. Maybe then I wouldn't be so afraid. I feel lost to know what an actual partnership is and what it looks like. This is uncharted territory. Maybe there isn't a blueprint for this kind of relationship.*

*I also think my idea of motherhood is when you lose yourself and any ambitions you may have but that's really untrue and unfair.*

*Love is not scarce... It is abundant...*

*If I am to be a mother or stepmother, I want to show up with love. Love for myself and love for them. Withholding love for Buck's kids doesn't make me independent. It just makes me cold.*

*I want them to witness a woman who takes care of herself and pursues her deepest desires. Because that is the kind of person I want them to be.*

The only wrong choice is to make one without love.

Mess

of shrapnel

an unrecognizable

makeshift

version of me


It's starting to fit together

to form a newness

that feels

nowhere near perfection


And with grand absurdity

it took me this long

to realize

that is the audacity

and the perfection of this

preposterous life

Remember

The ability to love your wreckage is always what God had intended.

You are your own parent now : be kind to yourself and be your best protector.

The ability to move despite your catastrophic stumbling is what a fearless woman does.

The world needs nothing from you but to fall in love with as many things as possible.

Start with yourself.

## Detour

I thought

I stumbled off the path

to dip my hands

in the icy water

to wash my palms of the

things that no longer served me


Fear kept me from returning


How relieving to realize

this

is the path

## Heavy Grace

is still Grace

# REIMAGINED CONCLUSION

Minutes back in Portland: 12

On NW 23rd and Pettygrove

Number of times I have walked past here: Hundreds

Sign says: Narcissistic Abuse Counseling

Times I have considered my marriage abusive: 0

"This is a type of love story where the happy ending lies in not finding Prince Charming. Rather, it lies in the realization that he never existed at all."

- Shahida Arabi, *POWER: Surviving and Thriving After Narcissistic Abuse*

The Diagnostic and Statistical Manual of Mental Disorders (5th ed.; DSM–5; American Psychiatric Association, 2013) defines a narcissistic person as indicating five (or more) of the following:

Has a grandiose sense of self-importance (i.e., exaggerates achievements and talents, expects to be recognized as superior without commensurate achievements)

Is preoccupied with fantasies of unlimited success, power, brilliance, beauty, or ideal love.

Believes that he or she is "special" and unique and can only be understood by, or should associate with, other special or high-status people (or institutions).

Requires excessive admiration.

Has a sense of entitlement (i.e., unreasonable expectations of especially favorable treatment or automatic compliance with his or her expectations).

Is interpersonally exploitative (i.e., takes advantage of others to achieve his or her own ends).

Lacks empathy: is unwilling to recognize or identify with the feelings and needs of others.

Is often envious of others or believes that others are envious of him or her.

Shows arrogant, haughty behaviors or attitudes.


Ex-husband's score : 9/9, a flawless performance.

Narcissist

noun.

x Deriving pleasure from another's pain.

x Sucking the soul out of another.

x Stealing my money and spirit.

x A mother-fucking leech.

  x A person I married.

## Narcissist's Greatest Hits

Love bombing

Idealization

Stone walling

Devaluation

Gaslighting

Triangulation


Check

Check

Check

Check

Check

Check

## Tab for the year

Nightmares ................................................................ 61

Panic attacks ............................................................ 5

Crying for no reason ............................................ 25

Crying with a reason ............................................ 42

Self-help books read ............................................ 13

Therapy sessions .................................................. 54

Times my therapist brought up codependency ........... 54

Times my therapist brought up narcissistic abuse ......... 0

Times I had to convince myself I was lovable ............... Every other day

Times I believed I had attracted this person

because I was inherently broken and lost ................... Every day

"Narcissistic abuse is unlike anything you've probably ever experienced...trauma made out of a million tiny shocks that shatter the memory, erode the self and break your life into fragments. It's psychological terrorism at its worst and confusing as hell at its best it hits the core of everything you once believed about the world...

When the victim is sufficiently hooked into the relationship and invested, that is when the tide turns, the false mask slips away, and the terror begins."

- Shahida Arabi, *POWER: Surviving and Thriving After Narcissistic Abuse*

What if



What if it was abuse?



What if

What if

none of it was my fault?

What if it was abuse?

What if I didn't enable someone

to treat me like shit

and tell me

I have nothing to offer the world?

What if nothing else mattered

except knowing

it wasn't my fault?

## Tab

Minutes spent reading the book cover to cover .................. 180

Minutes ran after reading .............................................. 60

Mile pace ................................................................. 7:15

Number of pedestrians I wanted to yell at for existing ......... 12

Emotional breakdown .................................................... 1

What if nothing else mattered

except knowing

it wasn't my fault?

Remember when you told me it was my fault when male students hit on me.

Remember when you told me my friends and family don't care about me.

Remember when you told me I was an alcoholic every chance you got cuz I got drunk on my birthday. Remember when you said that and you were getting high every week on meth and weed and drinking.

Remember when you told me I was wrong. All the fucking time.

Remember when you drove 100 miles an hour drunk at midnight and ran red lights and I begged you to stop.

Remember when you told me almost everything was my fault.

Remember when you tried to blow meth in my mouth.

Remember when you I covered for you coaching when you didn't show up.

Remember when you told me you didn't want my pussy and you definitely didn't want my ass.

Remember when you told me you got married because you knew I would leave if you didn't.

Remember when you told me you didn't want to get married in the first place.

Remember when you told me to move out. Then took it back, then told me again. Then told me that I was your best friend and the only person you can confide in.

Remember when you told me that no one knows the real me and the real me is unlovable.

Remember when we celebrated our one year anniversary at a soccer game and you wore the opposing team's jersey just to be an asshole and then spent the evening looking for weed with some 18-year-old kids that you help "mentor."

Remember when you told me it was wrong to talk about dismantling racism.

Remember when you told me I was selfish and cared too much about money and then took all my money and spent it on yourself.

Remember when you told me I was a flirt cuz I tried to talk and get to know your friends.

Remember when you quit your job cuz it was "too toxic." Remember when I worked at the exact same place and had to stick it out.

Remember when I worked several jobs to make ends meet while you were unemployed.

Remember when I was going to lunch with my friends I hadn't seen in years and you called me and made me come home.

Remember when you told me I had a sex problem.

Remember when you told me you were on Tinder just to talk with people.

Remember when you told me you were addicted to porn.

Remember when you told me you wanted to be a monk.

Remember when you told me you had a gun to your head in Mexico cuz the cartels thought you were your roommate... You pissed them off didn't you.

Remember when you neglected the dog and you dumped a can of corn into his bowl cuz you were getting high in the bedroom.

Remember when you left the dog in the car for hours cuz you were getting high with your friends.

Remember when you were supposed to take care of him and he got fleas and diarrhea.

Remember when you tried to take the dog and I told you no because I took care of him and paid for him and his food and the vet and I'll call the cops if you take him and you told me that was SO white to call the cops.

Remember when you told me that my waist wasn't as skinny as your ex-girlfriend's.

Remember when you told me I forced this life on you.

Remember after two months of marriage you told me you needed time away from me.

Remember when you told me that I didn't deserve to be greeted when I got home from earning money to pay for our home that you contribute nothing to.

Remember when you told me you weren't going to go to rehab or therapy.

Remember when I bent over backwards to make it work. To give you chances you didn't deserve.

Remember when you were under investigation for meth from the school district.

Remember when you told me you were confused when I asked for a divorce.

Remember when you were too busy to sign the papers.

Remember when you called me and told me you were going to kill yourself cuz of what I was doing.

Remember when I had to plea for a decision from the judge to fucking call it.

Remember when I told you to never contact me again and you did it anyway.

Remember when I had to block your number and you got a new number and texted me and I blocked you again.

Remember on what would have been our anniversary, our wedding song was playing through the windows outside of my apartment complex.

Remember when I had to move apartments cuz I was afraid you would stalk me and the dog.

Remember when you told me I was missed and if I wanted to talk to let you know.

Remember when I never let you know.

Remember when I beat myself up for a year believing I was somehow an enabler of your shittiness.

Remember when I told you you were being mean and you told me you wouldn't have to be that way if I was just "better."

Remember when I believed it was my codependency that got me involved with you. Not the fact that you're an abusive monster.

Remember when I was a good girl and didn't tell anyone what happened and never said one bad word about you or to you through the entire fucking thing.

Remember when I beat myself up believing I was somehow an enabler of your shittiness.

Remember when I believed it was my codependency that got me involved with you. Not the fact that you're an abusive monster.

The time is now to come forward with whatever killed your spark.

Remember when I was a good girl and didn't tell anyone what happened and never said one bad word about you or to you through the entire thing.

*Am I allowed to be angry now?*

God you're pathetic. You low-life, piece-of-shit, ridiculous, self-righteous, prick of an asshole. You have to build up your holier-than-though persona and build a following of children to "guide" when in fact you're such a broken piece of shit that you have to abuse and prey upon nice people like me. You used up ALL MY MONEY and told me I was too white. You told me I wasn't pretty, you told me I had a problem you told me that I was a flirt, that I was promiscuous, that I was sexually wrong. YOU ARE A MOTHERFUCKER. I was and am a normal human being. I am a woman who wanted to be loved and you destroyed my soul with your sadistic bullshit and fuckery about your "trauma" and "abuse" and "I'm the victim" blah blah blah. You loved bringing up your ex-girlfriend and watching me cry and lose it all the time. You disappear all the time because you are a spineless, total fucking monster. I know you were fucking other girls, watching porn, and on Tinder because you don't give a fuck about anyone but yourself.

You made me believe I was unlovable, that I was broken and tainted. Fuck the poems I wrote, fuck the vows, fuck your bullshit family, fuck your meth. I hope you die so you can stop sucking the soul from everyone around you like a fucking leech. Stop posturing yourself as a martyr and identifying with amazing people. You're a grade-A bullshitter that deserves to die in a fucking gutter. I wish the cartels would have killed you and I wish the malaria would have killed you. You're like Trump, you won't die cuz you're just too fucking evil. FUCK YOU FOR MAKING ME FEEL SCARED. I AM NOT AFRAID OF YOU ANYMORE. I AM NOT AFRAID OF LOVE FROM GOOD PEOPLE BECAUSE I AM A GOOD PERSON. I AM NOT AFRAID TO BE SEXY AND LIBERATED BECAUSE YOUR "LOVE" was manipulative and strangling. I hate you you motherfucker. I hate you I hate you. You can never take away my power. You can never take away my strength. No one can!!! I was afraid to be angry because I believed it was my fault. I'm fucking angry and will own that anger. I will own my power because you never had it in the first place.

I am the victim to have been ever been told by you I wasn't enough. You walked out on, shunned, belittled, and fucked with my mind, body and soul. Your abuse is fucking bullshit and I hate you for it. I hate hate hate you for it. I was taught to not hate but I HATE you.

## The Returning of Stuff

You can no longer
invade my dreams and stories
strangling my capacity to love
with dirty and unwashed hands

Have back the pain
you threw
as the dealer in a one-sided game

Keep the pipe and smoke
held more than my hand,
go back to the holes you hid in
and the lies that swarmed you

Take it all
I didn't ask for any of it in the first place

## A past that will no longer have me by the throat

"You're a flirt."—I am kind to people and give them my full attention.

"It's your fault that students hit on you."—My body and spirit are not landing spots for teenage hormones. They should be taught to respect women and have proper boundaries.

"My ex-girlfriend's waist was skinnier."—Real women don't compete to earn your bullshit validation. Real women are imperfect and in harmony with one another.

"I don't want your pussy and I definitely don't want your ass."—You're jealous of my ability to love and express love.

"You're so clingy. You're so obsessed with me."—You're the one who gets a job everywhere I work, you fucking idiot. You cling to my bank account, my car, and family.

"No one knows what you're really like."—The people around me understand and see that I am a genuinely kind and loving person.

"Your family and friends don't care about you."—My family and friends care deeply about me. They love me.

Novel Idea

THANK GOD

THANK GOD

he didn't ask me to stay

so that he would remain but a chapter

and not the whole book

# Reality

I am a warrior who was forged in the fire.

My beauty is all of me.

My body, mind, and spirit are mine—no one can take that from me.

I will never abandon myself because I am wiser, braver, and stronger.

I have so much to offer the world that you were disgustingly jealous of the whole time.

*At my brother's place after a run trying to hold it in.*

**Me**: Can I fall apart for a minute?

**My brother**: Of course.

December 24, 2020

*None of it was my fault. I didn't warrant, ask for, or attract this because I was broken....*

*I didn't co-create a toxic relationship with this person.*

*It wasn't because I was codependent. It was because he was abusive.*

*I think what is bothering me most about my therapist is that I believed somehow that I had fallen into the marriage because I wasn't in alignment with God.*

*I don't know if that is what she intended but it was certainly how I felt.*

*That I had forced this life upon myself because of my need to control everything.*

*I look back at posts and writings before my abuser and I was so confident and sure of myself.*

*Hell, I left my other boyfriend because I knew I where I was headed.*

*This relationship derailed me from a lot and it was because he was a bad person, not because I hadn't accepted God or Jesus into my heart.*

*How do you break up with your therapist when there was a huge miss on her part? Do you tell her? She's been really helpful and I've learned a lot about myself no doubt. This wasn't my parents' fault and their brokenness. It's not perfect, sure, but not to attract abuse onto me. No one asks for this.*

*This person deliberately abused me.*

"The first recipe for happiness is:

avoid too lengthy meditation on the past."

- André Maorois

I AM WORTHY OF LOVE AND ADORATION

GENUINE PEOPLE CARE GENUINELY ABOUT ME

EVERYTHING FEAR-BASED IS AN ILLUSION

I AM POWERFUL

I AM LOVED

THERE ARE MIRACLES HAPPENING ALL AROUND ME

Abundance

Crawl out from that place

you've been hiding

where scarcity and lack line the walls

Walk towards

this celestial

madness

and catch all the love that will fall

December 2020 - July 2021

But what if I forgave him?

Would that help me to forgive myself?

He greatly disappointed me. And I disappointed myself by being involved in a terrible situation.

The stars aligned for a perfect storm. He doesn't deserve to die. That won't fix my hurt. I feel so bad for him that he won't ever live up to his potential. Deep down, his abuse comes from a hollow feeling of unlovability. He disappointed everyone in his life and may never be the person he wanted to be. He was capable of a lot. There was a lot of good which I can choose to see. Take all the lessons, the good and the bad. He was and is sick.

Separate the soul of a person, their trauma, their addictions.

Forgive them as a person and forgive yourself.

I don't want to be angry, vengeful, or regret anything. You took the expedited crash course in life lessons - you are wiser and more peaceful for it.

When I look back at that time of my life I will

-Be grateful that it is no longer my life.

-Appreciate the lessons that came from it.

-Remember that life is hard and everyone suffers, we must continue to find the joy.

-You will never have to feel that way again.

It was after a long walk

through a haunted graveyard

where ghosts and old stories dwelled

that compassion laid herself to sleep


While she rested

forgiveness crept

quietly in

and carried away the

suffocating burden

of resentment


Oh what a feeling to breathe again

"Fear, to a great extent, is born of a story we tell ourselves, and so I chose to tell myself a different story from the one women are told. I decided I was safe. I was strong. I was brave."

- Cheryl Strayed, *Wild: From Lost to Found on the Pacific Crest Trail*

# Spell

These are the words

This is the verse

This is the love

To shatter my curse

    This is the poem

    This is the bell

    This is the light

    To shake me from hell

        This is the hook

        This is the tell

        This is the light

        That whispers a spell

            This is the story

            This is the verse

            This is the moment

            My love will disperse

                This is the book

                This is the verse

                This is the birth

                Of a new universe

# Belief

I am safe

I am whole

Everything I need is already inside me

I need to let my love happen

## Power

The power of a storm that

splendors the ocean

to wrestle and wave

colors of indigo and turquoise

to new shapes

and virgin depths...

If we harness that power

and hold it in our bodies

we'll move the way

blue fire marches to the sky

December 26, 2020

*I now know that I am allowed to love and live my life.*

For the reality of what life will look like

After a dark night of

rattling walls

and rainfall on the roof

I stepped outside

to see

the ground

glistening

and the green trees

and the yellow flowers

and the pink houses

and I watched

the Earth shine

bright for all to see

You'll know it is the correct path

because it is marked

with love

*On a hike with Buck on Christmas Eve*

**Me**: I guess what I am saying is that I've figured out a lot recently and I'm ready to love you. Like really ready to love you.

**Buck**:

**Me**: Are you crying?

**Buck**: Of course dear.

December 26, 2020

1-year anniversary card from Buck

*Dearest Maureendear,*

*I'm so thankful that I "met" you a year ago and that you have become an interwoven thread that keeps my life tight. The past year has been the most awakening thing for me. I've realized how special and lucky I feel to have you in my life. You have made me healthier physically, mentally, spiritually. Your discipline, enthusiasm, curiosity, and fervor for life are infectious to be around. Your commitment to self-healing and discovery is inspiring to me and others. You make me be who I want to be and show through your daily actions that you won't let anything or anyone stop you form living your best life, and I'm down with that.*

*You are perfectly imperfect and I know God loves me because he gave me you.*

## Love

Envelop me like the

sun on the budding flower

I'll catch you like water

with leaves stretched wide

Seep into my roots

and call me to rise

# INTIMATE REVOLUTION

sunbeams laid resting as

rainbow roads

of purple and pinks

moved through the air


the sky

she grieved

for she was not *blue* like the sea


she oohd and ahd

when the light came up

and she watched the water glisten


oh if shed known

she was looking at her own reflection

look at what you have overcome

look at what we have all overcome

if there was ever a time to ohh and ahh

it is now

staring at your own reflection

"When she does not find love, she may find poetry.

Because she does not act, she observes, she feels, she records; a color, a smile awakens profound echoes within her; her destiny is outside her, scattered in cities already built, on the faces of men already marked by life, she makes contact, she relishes with passion and yet in a manner more detached, more free, than that of a young man... The young girl throws herself into things with ardor, because she is not yet deprived of her transcendence; and the fact that she accomplishes nothing, that she is nothing, will make her impulses only the more passionate. Empty and unlimited, she seeks from within her nothingness to attain All."

- Simone de Beauvoir, *The Second Sex*

## delusional

I asked for a typewriter for my 8th birthday

but I am not a writer

I have written in my diary everyday since 5th grade

but I am not a writer

I was the editor of my school paper

but I am not a writer

I taught English and writing and was paid for that

but I am not a writer

my computer and notebooks are filled with poems

but I am not a writer

## power ballad

tyrants fear the poet

a poem only dwells

in the heart of a magician

goodness

cannot be

bought

nor stolen

the tyrant will hurl gunshots to the air

and spit fireworks from a barrel

the poet will breathe a pink sky

to set the sun on his violence

he'll roar the cry of a coward–

a tantrum to be let in

he knows it's almost midnight

on his ephemeral reign

but only a poet can open the window

that hangs on the wall of knowing

she'll open it and sing of sanctity

then merely whisper

and the galaxy will hold her words

forever

**remembered dreams**

how wild I grew

when I weeded my past

and gave my spirit

a chance

to breathe

January 4, 2021

*"When did you learn you had to pay a big price for the things you want?*

*You don't have to pay a big price for the things you want.*

*You think there's more power in the struggle...*

*Allow yourself to want something and then open your circuit.*

*I could never get sick enough to help others get well.*

*You are a vibration.*

*Don't face reality. Create reality.*

*If you wait for something to happen then you are conditionally loving life.*

*Everything is right on track."*

- Abraham Hicks

## flood lights

I used to think

I was so broken

I needed caging

so I wouldn't self-destruct

but for certain, my love

is not     meant     to     be     contained

but

    spread and

    shared

like a light

through a glass chandelier

that permeates through its prisms

every

side

of a

million

  crystals

### growing SPIRIT

pick up the ground

as the ground has held you


smell the roots

smell the soil

and remember

last years fallen leaves

are this years radical nourishment


fall in love with

your own body's existence –

          she endured a brittle winter

and melted into

a gorgeous

(deeply)

over-due

spring

## the emerald city

ask me and I will show you

how tall trees of

emerald moss and vines that hang

like soft jewelry

are the sweet reminders

of how small and made up

our lives really are

I promise I will show you

how to rejoice when

the wet clay clings

to our feet and we move

and we move

and we move

maybe

I will even show you

how to find the sun

through thick grey rolling

clouds and twisting

branches that beat us

to the light

but at the very least

I will show you

that the remedy

for hollow intimacy is in

the breath of the earth's

quiet melody

January 24, 2021

*1 day away from 30*

*Goodbye years of wandering without lust.*

*Wondering how to fit my strangely*

*shaped body, spirit, and mind into something*

*palatable and familiar.*

*Goodbye to a version of me that had to transform*

*into a cocoon of self-doubt and fear.*

*They wrapped me tight...*

*How naive to think it was safety.*

*Hello to a decade of doing precisely what I want.*

*Joy will define this decade.*

# space

take it up with your voice and your words

that you deliberately uncensored

so loudly it thunders grey skies to blue

take it up with your hips

and your handles

and head full of rebellion

and watch as the world pays homage

take it up with your opinions and descent

that hang in the air like

a clock at the stroke of midnight

time is up

you must show us

that life is absurd

when set fiery ablaze

you are far from smoke and mirrors

you are real in god's gaze

March 1, 2021

*I had a dream my grandmother was smiling and giddy and playful.*

*I never knew her to be that way in real life.*

*She was always so well-mannered and contained.*

the good   +   powerful

power is not impressive nor boastful,
but ephemeral and rare

the applause of lightening
before it hears thunder

it is seeking the beauty in all nooks,
windowsills, and forgotten alleys

the stadium's loud roar before
the whistle has even blown

a simple question
what would god have me learn today

the voices of people
that march towards a new world
before they've ever seen it

the song you don't just hear
but feel in your chest

the insanity of the unyielding
pursuit for simple understanding

trusting the uncertainty
of defending even
our darkest decisions

how pleasantly wrong I had been this whole time

joy fell awake

after a full day of lounging in the sun

the cool night air remembered her smile

joy

you have permission to come alive now

you have permission to sing

## moonshine

in day light

we may see her—

perfectly round

unremarkable

unnoticeable


the spell begins

when the well

of the sun runs dry

and leaves the sky

to rest


but here


in the darkness,


what stunning bliss—


ah

we can finally see

how brightly

one moon can sing

## simple surplus

the beauty of these days
is that it always feels the same—
yet everything has changed

it's the same poem as always
because these days—
goodness is simple

these days the
surprise of a red sky
fills me better than the
echoes of an empty glass
in a crowded bar

it's the same poem
that was never broken—
just ignored
for more ridiculous things

this might be the same poem
about the same twisted branches
of the oak tree my neighbor tamed
and sweet stars that hang
like ornaments in the night

so I'll beat its drum
and sing with a pen
to celebrate the sameness
that is in the
wandering
for simplicity

I'll write you the same poem
about the dew on a blade of grass,
and how it feels to walk
with the sun—
as if I haven't been doing this
everyday
for what feels like eternity

the slow walk with my mother

the soft waves that make you laugh and run towards warmer sand

migos's yawns

the breath you remind yourself to take

my brother's unkept beard

my sister's gentle hands

the pen on paper

my dad's sarcasm

the bench near the river

 and the ring I chucked in it

the scent of snowfall

the smell of spring

the letters to and from a human

the whispered I love you

the post-it that reads: heavy grace

the voice note that reminds me that everything I need is already inside me


the feeling of peace when I remember it always has been

**how to say goodbye**

when you say goodbye it must

be done

slowly

over many            many years

we cannot forget

that one day

we will say goodbye

and all it will be is me

again

and always

# EPILOGUE

## for the good girls

reimagine conclusions and

shatter

 your delusions


through spiritual effusions

breathe in

a transfusion

that propels

your evolution


this is a rebellion turned

revo

fucking

lution

A very special thank you to those that helped actualize this book.

My guardian angel, best friend, and copy editor Carolynne. I have no words that will do justice the grace and love you have shown me. Thank you.

Joanne Sprott, the kindest editor that ever lived. Thank you for seeing me and my story. Your notes made me giggle and cry.

Kelsey Hones, Tamika Abaka-Wood and my employer B+A who championed this journey and book. You believed in me when I had nothing to give and walked with me while I healed.

Robi Wood, my first reader and sage.

Buck Tufty who bragged to people I was writing a book 10 months before I even started.

When I started writing this book in November of 2020, I had no idea what I was doing. I have whole body sobbed while writing this and when I started to finish it a year later, I full body sobbed again because I actually fucking wrote it.

Since leaving off in March 2021, I am energized by a new chapter, Through these last few years, our relationships have strengthened and become more intimate and honest than I could have ever imagined. A very special thank you to my brother who was my sobriety catalyst, I am proud of you, and us.

When I think back to where I was when I met my ex-husband, I no longer feel embarrassed or shameful, I feel compassion. Compassion for a young woman who was earnest to do the right things and fell into a devastating situation. I am lucky to have the support systems and resources I had while recovering, I know not everyone is afforded those same privileges.

I hope my criticism of the patriarchy does not come across as men bashing. They are also victims in this system and I dream of a world where these social viruses such as the patriarchy, white supremacy, and capitalism are shattered illusions we discuss with shock and horror in history books.

My first draft of this book was polished and consisted of only poems that allowed me to stay at arms length from the subject. I was extremely concerned with people taking me seriously as a writer. I just hadn't accepted that part of me yet. Then a good friend pointed out that I was still being a good girl with my writing, so it became a messy scrapbook. This style is not for everyone, but it helped me to unlock my creativity and to heal immensely. So please be nice.

My work now is to liberate joy and creativity to uncover our truest, deepest selves. I desire a world where systems, ideas, and narratives are designed to allow humanity to thrive.

I know now more than ever that by allowing things in your life to die, you make room for love and experiences you never even fathomed. I was "lucky" in a sense to be forced into a corner, forced to heal in order to survive. I hope that this story helps others heal from their own trauma, and to remember that pain is not permanent. There are magical possibilities if we work to remove our spiritual bondage and choose to really live.

If you have made it this far and are still reading then holy shit...

Thank you for seeing me.

Love,

Maureen

*People and books I owe a great deal of healing to. My deepest gratitude.*

*While they may not have been mentioned in this book, I had many mentors in the form of books. I am so grateful to these writers for sharing stories of courage and love.*

*A Course in Miracles*

Eckhart Tolle, *A New Earth*

Marianna Williamson, *A Return to Love*

Henry Cloud and John Townsend, *Boundaries*

Shahida Arabi, *POWER: Surviving and Thriving After Narcissistic Abuse: A Collection of Essays on Malignant Narcissism and Recovery from Emotional Abuse*

David Brooks, *The Road to Character,*

Simone De Beauvoir, *The Second Sex*

Jordan Kisner, *Thin Places*

Annie Grace, *This Naked Mind*

Jia Tolentino, *Trick Mirror*

Glennon Doyle, *Untamed,*

Cheryl Strayed, *Wild*

Jackson McKenzie, *Whole Again*

Simone De Beauvoir, *The Second Sex*

To checkout more of Maureen's work, deep dive into momofitz.com

*If you are experiencing, or suspect you are experiencing an abusive relationship, please seek help at*

*thehotline.org*

*or call 1-800-799-SAFE.*